Gene,

May The Lord Bless The Work
of Your Hands. May He Reward
Your efforts.

I thank You For The Curiosity
You show — it makes People feel
Valued, Seen + Heart.

Pope.

DECISION
DESIGN

A BELIEVER'S GUIDE TO THE LIFE YOU ARE CALLED TO LIVE

TASHER ADAAREWA

WESTBOW
PRESS®
A DIVISION OF THOMAS NELSON
& ZONDERVAN

This book is a work of non-fiction. Unless otherwise noted, the author
and the publisher make no explicit guarantees as to the accuracy of
the information contained in this book and in some cases, names
of people and places have been altered to protect their privacy.

WestBow Press books may be ordered through booksellers or by contacting:

WestBow Press
A Division of Thomas Nelson & Zondervan
1663 Liberty Drive
Bloomington, IN 47403
www.westbowpress.com
844-714-3454

Scripture quotations are taken from the New King James Version®. Copyright
© 1982 by Thomas Nelson. Used by permission. All rights reserved.

ISBN: 978-1-6642-6483-0 (sc)
ISBN: 978-1-6642-6482-3 (hc)
ISBN: 978-1-6642-6484-7 (e)

Library of Congress Control Number: 2022907763

Print information available on the last page.

WestBow Press rev. date: 05/05/2022

For Prisca,
whose decisions made this possible.
Thank you.

CONTENTS

INTRODUCTION

"In the beginning, God created the heavens and the earth." (Genesis 1:1) The rest of Genesis 1 is a clinic as an architect pulls together a masterpiece. Though the Lord does what only He can do, create something out of nothing, His approach is a perfect template for anyone who wants to build something. Whether your goal is an extraordinary life, having an enduring marriage, a close-knit and wonderful family, or a great business, the how-to that can guarantee success is in that first chapter.

Consider, for example, the order in which He speaks things into being. It was deliberate. Look at those six days *backwards*. God created man in "Our likeness," intent from the start to give them dominion over the earth and everything He made. Therefore, He needed to make the fish of the sea, the birds of the air, the cattle, and every creeping thing first. Would it have made any sense to make man then figure out where he would live and what he would eat?

We understand photosynthesis, osmosis and many of the processes that take place in and around plants so that they can grow and produce fruit. All of these living things need food, which is why on the third day before He had created any animals, He commanded the earth to bring forth grass, the herb that yields seeds and the fruit tree that produces according to its kind. By the third day, God had already commanded the light, the dry ground and the water to be in place.

Genesis 1 shows a sequential approach with God providing what would sustain each creature before speaking it into existence so that nothing would suffer want. He had a vision of what He wanted things to look like, and from there, He worked backwards. It was not a haphazard push and pull and see what would happen. He was deliberate with each step. God is a God of systems, rules and order. He wrote laws of gravity and aerodynamics, progressive overload, specific adaptation to imposed demand, and many others we have yet to codify. It was into all of this that God created humanity and gave us dominion over it.

From the verse, "let us make man in our own image and let him have dominion" (v.26), we know God had a purpose for creating us. Similarly, He has a specific part for all of us to play. While things like where you are from and your race factors confer certain disproportionate advantages and challenges, the things that can help us reach God's best are equally distributed. His salvation, completed on the cross, is freely given to everyone. The call is, "if any of you lacks wisdom, let him ask (James 1:5)." Time ticks along at the same pace so that we all have 24 hours in a day. Jesus said the Father in heaven makes His sun rise on the evil and good and sends rain on the just and the unjust (Matthew 5:45). Our ability to extract and exercise these things that the Lord gives liberally to all will determine the quality of life we lead.

God's call on your life is unique, and He has left it to you to build it. Decision design is about the architect- you. Any professional who understands their craft gathers the material he needs before starting because preparation is as integral to the outcome as the process. The quality of this preparation and the process of putting them together distinguishes the outstanding from the average. Ultimately, God has predestined you for adoption (Ephesians 1:5) to conform to the image of His Son (Romans 8:29), that you might obtain an inheritance (Ephesians 1:11). However, the life He has called you to live before His glorious return is one you will have to construct. Whether you hear, "Well done good and faithful servant," depends on your decisions. This book is about helping you understand, prepare for and make choices that you can look on with pride. The chapters deal with the environment in which decisions happen, the steps before and after, and the decision's elements. Decisions do not occur in a vacuum, and they always impact others. There are sections dedicated to people decisions-those involved in your journey, how they can help (Chapter 8) and how to communicate with them, including resolving conflict (Chapter 6).

The brain, lauded as the most complex organ in all of creation derives, sees the execution of decisions and then evaluates them. Several chapters (5, 10, 12) expand on its operation. How does it formulate questions, weigh out its options and protect you? What role does emotion play (Chapter 5, 18,19)? How do you decide which way to go (Chapters 6 and 13) when you have to compromise?

Jewish teacher, Daniel Lapin, notes that the word "good" is used seven times during the seven days of creation as God expresses His satisfaction with the various parts of the world He has spoken into being and man whom He has formed. The eighth time He uses the word, God focuses on the universal and eternal symbol of money—gold.[1]

If the medium and result of commerce received God's commendation, business certainly could too. God does not outlaw trade or profit. He gives direction to govern how His people conduct themselves when they engage in business. In fact, in the parable of the talents, it was partly because the behaviour of the slothful servant denied his master the chance to get a profit that he deserved the darkness. (Matthew 25:14-30) Business, done right, serves its Creator. The principles that govern it echoes His word and its impact on individuals and the community is positive.

Gold is on the periodic table, a proxy for science. The elements encapsulate everything we have discovered in the physical world. Physics, mechanics, engineering and medicine all work around our understating of these elements and the compounds they form when they combine. Psychology is of primary consideration as it is the study of human behaviour, how we think, feel and ultimately interact with other people and the environment. Once more, as the handiwork of God, the study of all these things, which God said were *good* when He first made them, should reveal His thoughts. The conclusions and recommendations of science also ought to be in lockstep with God's revealed word. The Creator explained the water cycle millennia ago in Ecclesiastes: "All the rivers run into the sea, yet the sea is not full; to the place from which the rivers come, there they return again." (Ecclesiastes 1:7) Psychotherapies build on the impact of thoughts on our perspectives, decisions, actions and even our physical health. This approach is an extension of the scripture, "as he thinks in his heart, so is he." (Proverbs 23:7)

This book harnesses concepts from these two servants of God: business and science, to explore the idea of *decision design*. It will explain how to think about decisions, which one to make and which ones to leave alone, thus minimising regret. Abraham's life serves as the canvas for discussing decision design. Each chapter uses some aspect of his behaviour or dissects some decisions he made, drawing lessons to imitate and avoid.

The book is for believers and followers of Christ. Followers of Christ take His Word as law, like the very breath of life. And while He doesn't force us to obey, we do so because we believe His direction will take us to the highest He has for us. This book assumes you aspire to reach your full potential in Him. The ideas discussed take these as a given.

Decision Design is an integration of the Word of God with scientific and business observations. The integration of these three forms the frameworks for thinking and practical steps for the believer who wants to be the architect of his own life.

1

CALLING AND PURPOSE

Now the LORD had said to Abram: "Get out of your country, from your family and from your father's house to a land that I will show you. I will make you a great nation; I will bless you and make your name great, and you shall be a blessing. I will bless those who bless you, and I will curse him who curses you, and in you, all the families of the earth shall be blessed." (Genesis 12:1-3)

There can be no doubt that God called Abram to walk with Him as a friend. This invitation is the simplest and most important part of the entire story. It is the declaration Jesus makes in the book of Revelation, "Behold I stand at the door and knock." (Revelation 3:20) It is the voice of the beloved who knocks, saying, "Open for me, my sister, my love." (Song of Songs 5:2) In today's imagery, it is looking at your phone as it vibrates, ringing with God's name on the caller ID. He wants to talk, to be in a relationship with you.

Called By Name

It is easy to miss the incredible blessing in this simplicity if you go straight to the secondary issues. What is my calling? What gifts do I have? These are secondary issues. The first thing to note is that God has called you, a distinction that is foundational to the outcome of the entire journey. You will feel discouraged, tired, and need rest as you walk in that calling. Sometimes sleep, and refreshment will not come. It may be that some task or project is not going well and seems hopeless. It may even be after seeking God repeatedly. You feel your prayers are going nowhere, and situations are not changing. It is not uncommon to wonder if you are on the right path. Should you stay? What good will it do you to persist?

Think about the Enemy's original approach to Eve. (Genesis 3:1) He suggested that she was incomplete, that God was holding her back, and that her level, position, and status were not what they could be because of it. He cast doubt over her view of the situation. He attacked her mind with words aimed at her thinking process and understanding. With that, Satan corrupted the purpose of the commandments of God in her eyes and of God Himself. He is still a thief who comes to steal, kill, and destroy- will he be gentler now? (John 10:10) He is subtle- the way people talk to you, what they say, whether they pass you over for a promotion, withhold a raise or squeeze you out of a deal. When you know that your church or recreational sports team members go to social events and invite each other to dinner, and you never get an invitation. Moreover, they can't make it whenever you offer to host- there is much in how things happen that chips away at how you see yourself.

The one unshakable thought you can trust in times like these is, "The Lord said." There is an incredible amount to bolster your confidence, self-esteem, and self-worth if you can believe God chose you.

Jesus' teaching is a part of this puzzle we must factor in. "Many are called, but few are chosen." (Matthew 22:14) There are several concepts to unpack in parsing out what He intended when He said this. To begin with, if it is true God formed each of us in our mothers' wombs, then it is true that every one of us, believer or not, is his. Indeed, being the Creator, everything in creation is His. The intricacies of each person, with unique fingerprints, a one-in-the-universe combination of genetic material and everything that comes with that, are the result of God's precise time, effort, love, and power. That you are alive is a matter of intention. He called you into existence with a specific design and plan so that you can contribute to His story and His glory.

The second level of calling found in the Jewish view of Abram's story suggests there was nothing special about Abram the man. Indeed, the Bible does not distinguish him from his father or ancestors. They were all idol worshippers. The invitation from God, in Jewish tradition, was to many, to everyone. Abram chose himself in that he alone answered the call.[1] He stepped forward, prepared to leave behind what was familiar to follow a single, invisible God. According to one of those stories passed down from generation to generation, Abram's father, Terah, owned a shop that sold idols. Abraham could not accept that these idols possessed any powers, so he destroyed them. At once, Abraham stood alone, an individual and the first Jew. The original Hebrew word for Hebrew means "one who crosses over." In other words, his badge of pride and very identification mean willingness and ability to transform himself from someone who stands on one side of a matter to someone entirely different who takes quite a divergent approach.

A similar level of calling is the one we see in the redemption of the children of Israel from Pharaoh's grip. God declared them His son, His people, a holy nation, and a kingdom of priests. (Exodus 19:6) He performed wonders that had never been seen or heard of before or since. After four hundred years of tears for God's deliverance, when the time finally came for Israel to inherit the land promised to Abram, they crumbled with fear. Hebrews said they did not mix the word with faith (Hebrews 4:2) and missed what God had in store for them. Of the hundreds of thousands, if not a million, people who came out of Egypt, only two made it into the land of milk and honey. "Surely none of the men who came up from Egypt, from twenty years old and above, shall see the land of which I swore to Abraham, Isaac, and Jacob because they have not wholly followed Me." (Numbers 32:11)

— The key is in the words of the Lord Himself; the promise was only to those who followed. From a nation called, only two responded appropriately. It was the mercy and justice of God and the love He had for Abraham to fulfil His promise that allowed those below nineteen years to enter Canaan.

— The key here is to recognize you have been called, and by your response, you can choose to walk with God. The Gospel of John teaches the same thing. The Word became flesh and lived among men… because God so loved the entire world, with everyone in it. But it was only to them that received Him that He gave them the right to be the sons and daughters of God. (John 1:12, 14) Choose this day whom you will serve.

Why Call Me?

— What did God call Abram to do? Walk with Him. Why? Herein
— lies the secondary issue. God wanted to be in a relationship, and in choosing to be a part of that, Abram would reach the highest and experience the best of all God had planned for him—he would be the father of a nation, a race, of all believers. As with Abram, what God needed to bring out that plan was already in Abram when He called him. He needed Abram's seed. When the time came, that seed would become Isaac, Israel, Judah and… Jesus—God's means of blessing every family on the earth.

The same was true for Moses. While he groped in the dark for some excuse to back out of his life's mission, God told him it was time. Moses misdiagnosed what was needed to do the work that God was calling him to. He thought status (Who am I that

I should go?), credibility (Suppose they do not believe me...) and eloquence (I am not eloquent!) were the tools needed. God was looking for humility, a servant's heart, someone who had seen the affliction of His people and had a burning desire for justice and righteousness. Gideon, Samuel, Jeremiah, Isaiah, and many others all considered one thing, while God's requirement was something else altogether.

God has not called you to a task you are ill-suited. When He says, "Come" or "Go," He has given you the credentials you need to do it by those exact words. God has ever sent no one without Him going with the person. Those who have responded to His call have never reported that God abandoned them along the way. He has never given any commandment He expects us to do independently. To be called by God is to be invited into collaboration with Him. To have gifts from Him is to be allowed to wield something of His so you can participate in what He plans to do. To be called is the privilege of having the Almighty God, who does not need help from anyone, lay down His omnipotence to act through you, with you and for you. God intended for you to use whatever gifts you have to bless others. It is only in doing so that you can reach your highest potential. When you get that, God is glorified.

"I, the LORD, have called You in righteousness, and will hold Your hand; I will keep You and give You as a covenant to the people ... I am the LORD, that is My name and My glory I will not give to another, nor My praise to carved images." (Isaiah 42:5-8)

This is then the secondary issue—it is not a question of Whether you have any gifts or if your life has a purpose. The challenge is understanding you cannot be anything but called and gifted because the reason for all that is non-negotiable: to give God the glory. Isaiah's passage breaks it down, "I called you by your name; You are Mine. When you pass through the waters, I will be with you... Everyone who is called by My name, Whom I have created for My glory, I have formed him, yes, I have made him." (Isaiah 43:1, 2, 8)

Consider the absurdity of calling someone deaf and mute on the phone. You would be better off trying some other means of communicating if you will avoid frustration. Similarly, would an Almighty, omniscient God call someone who could not respond? Would He choose someone for an assignment they could not possibly perform?

How Do I Do That?

What Isaiah captured in this chapter leads us to the tertiary issue—the most important question of your life. How am I (equipped) to give God the glory?

These steps from primary to tertiary illustrate the first point of better decision-making. The more complex the decision you must make, the more imperative it is to change your question from a simple yes and no format (closed question) to a what or how question. The former is a search for confirmation. It is much like a search engine, an incredibly powerful algorithm written to give you everything that most closely matches the query you entered. They are confirmation devices. In contrast, because they ask about implementation, what and how questions, they are less likely to tell you what you want to hear. They engage the brain in problem-solving mode.

Revisiting the Lord's words to Abram, what was He calling him to do? It was to be a conduit, the passage through which God would deliver blessings to the world. Abram would exemplify what God wants for you: a close relationship with Him and an assignment among your contemporaries.

2

SETTING A VISION

Now the LORD had said to Abram: "Get out of your country, from your family and from your father's house to a land that I will show you. I will make you a great nation; I will bless you and make your name great, And you shall be a blessing. I will bless those who bless you, And I will curse him who curses you; And in you, all the families of the earth shall be blessed." (Genesis 12:1-3)

In these words, God does not just call Abram. He does not just make promises. God sets a vision for Abram, guiding his life and choices from that point on. Understanding what happened at this point sets up the rest of the discussion on decision design. God's words are keys that unlock hidden dreams and breathe hope that visions can be a reality. Imbued with this newfound aspiration, Abraham also has something that will push and pull him to something beyond his wildest dreams.

Passion and Prospecting

Imagine, for a moment, your ideal life. Without limiting yourself to what may or may not be possible, what falls within the confines of reality or what might be embarrassing if someone else found out about it, go ahead and dream. What do you picture when you think about the abundance for which Jesus came and died? Who is there with you? What are you doing? No doubt what you d is in the future. With just a few prompts, you were able to remove some things from your current life and add others to meet that definition of ideal. This ability to take an abstract concept (the future!) and simulate it in your mind is what psychologists call prospecting.[1] You have pre-experienced the future.

For Abram, already wealthy, the image of a son and heir dominated that vision. In it, he was free from the crushing pressure and practices that went with worshipping molten idols. Never would those dreams extend to descendants, numbering like the sand on the seashore or the stars in the sky. He might have envisioned vast land for his livestock to graze, but that would never stretch to reach an entire country. Man's ideal, our highest thoughts pale to God's, of which "no eye has seen, no ear has heard, and it has not entered into the heart of men what God has prepared for those who love Him." (1 Corinthians 2:9) Up until that point, Abram had lived, done okay by the day's standard, but he was living well below his purpose. What God said to Abram was just what he needed. For the Lord to speak to Abram in a way that would move him into a response, God spoke to his deepest desire. If He had promised him livestock and a wife, Abram would not need to move from where he was. He already had those things. To hear about his seed, to hear God wanted to take something in him and use it to bless all the families of the earth—that intrigued him.

The same was true for Moses when he met the Lord in the burning bush. (Exodus 2:11-3:22) At that point, he was married, had sons, and took care of his father-in-law's sheep. God was calling him, not just to an absence of the peace he was enjoying at that time but to uncomfortable situations. He was calling him to return to the land he had fled to save his life. Yet, Moses was the most qualified for the job because God wanted someone whose fire would burn at injustice. He wanted someone who hurt at the state of his people but would also have the patience to shepherd them as he was doing the sheep. Chances are, if God wanted Moses to go back to operate on the state's politics, Moses would not have had the same passion.

Discovering your vision

The literature on developing a vision is voluminous. Most businesses and a fair amount of the population at an individual level have a dream, yet not everyone reaches the heights they set out to achieve. So how can you set yours up and attain it? How can you decipher and raise to God's plan for you? Research suggests there are specifics to a compelling vision and how you develop it that can increase the chances of growth in that direction. As you think about yours, consider the following.

When you think of that abundant life, the future you envision should remind you about or help you create your sense of purpose. Remember, it is not a matter of not having a purpose as a Christian, but how you are uniquely gifted to bring glory to your Creator. When what you dream of is infused with your purpose, there is evidence it might lead to a longer life[4] with increased career commitment over time.[5] It may be challenging to figure out where to start, but God has not left that area unaddressed. The callings of Abram and Moses suggested that the things you yearn for are God-given keys to help you find that specific purpose for your life. God planted a deep desire in a man and his barren wife. He intended to use that deep desire to bring them closer to Himself, and in walking with Him, He would meet that need. Moses wanted justice and peace, whether the altercation was between fellow Jews or a Jew and an Egyptian. Jesus took advantage of the skills and passions of fishermen and turned them into fishers of men.

To begin understanding what you have been called to, examine your unique combination of desires. Think about:

> - What excites you?
> - What makes you angry?
> - What do you feel a deep desire to start, correct, or end? What would it be if you had a $1 million cheque you could give to any cause?
> - How would you spend it if you were free of other obligations and could volunteer unlimited time?
> - If you could solve one or two problems in the world, what would they be?
> - What challenge, if fixed, would make the world better overnight?
> - What issues make you (want to) cry out to God?
> - What are you excited to do away with when Jesus returns that makes you desperate for that second advent?

Questions such as these, designed to get you thinking about your "dreams, aspirations and fantasies", hopefully, align deeply with your core identity, values, and goals. This is important for hope to arise,[6,9] the first of many positive emotions needed to move toward God's ideal for you. It is what you are free to have, to be and to enjoy because God willed it for you. This ideal is in contrast with a life lived out of obligation. It is the path you end up on when you do what you must, should and have to. To be sure, following God's ideal may entail giving up good things. Recall the story of David and Jonathan.

Promotion and Prevention

Now when he had finished speaking to Saul, the soul of Jonathan was knit to the soul of David, and Jonathan loved him as his own soul. Saul took him that day and would not let him go home to his father's house anymore. Then Jonathan and David made a covenant because he loved him as his own soul. And Jonathan took off the robe that was on him and gave it to David, with his armour, even to his sword and his bow and his belt. (1 Samuel 18:1-4)

The stripping of Jonathan's armour was symbolic. Jonathan recognised the anointing in David's life and aligned himself with him. If David took over, Jonathan would not inherit the kingdom. In those days, tradition has it that kings often eradicated the line of those they had usurped, lest there be young men left who could marshal uprisings when they got older. Saul was thinking about this when he criticised Jonathan for loving David.

Then Saul's anger was aroused against Jonathan, and he said to him, "You son of a perverse, rebellious woman! Do I not know that you have chosen the son of Jesse to your own shame and to the shame of your mother's nakedness? For as long as the son of Jesse lives on the earth, you shall not be established, nor your kingdom. Now, therefore, send and bring him to me, for he shall surely die." (1 Samuel 20:30-31)

Following God's plan will mean leaving some things behind. Those who feel you should hold on to them will not be pleased. Unfortunately, these are often parents. Both Joseph and David had their brothers mock, belittle, and try to silence them. Others who are close to you, well-meaning in their approach, will prove themselves obstacles to moving forward.

In most cases, however, discouragement comes from the inside. It comes from your doubts and fears. Whereas the ideal life and the ideal you are defined and buoyed by the freedom bought by Jesus, the average unfulfilled life is characterised by fear. Where God says nothing is impossible because nothing is too hard for Him, the perspective that dominates is the one full of negativity. You were hurt before, tried before, and it did not work out; you do not have the credentials, etc. Boyatzis and Akrivou[9] warn that working toward that person your parents, siblings, friends or the fearful you want you to be will lead to feelings of betrayal, frustration, and anger. These come up when you realise you have wasted time and energy pursuing someone else's dreams and expectations, that you have spent your life on things that hold no passion for you.

Psychologists also contend that for a vision to be effective—to inspire you enough to lead to lasting change—the things your ideal self looks toward must be promotion rather than prevention-focused. A vision is more powerful when it causes you to reach for something rather than make changes to avoid something. Promotion describes growth, change and gain, while prevention focuses on keeping things the same. Or should there be any change, it is about what you will lose or not lose. It is the difference between walking through the desert toward the Promised Land, eating manna along the way, or wishing you were back under the harsh conditions of slavery, but at least you had fish freely, along with cucumbers, melons, leeks, the onions, and the garlic. (Numbers 11:5) For a vision to be compelling, you must be willing to leave behind what you already have in the hope of reaching something better. If Abram had gotten stuck on the leave your country and your father's house part, he would have missed becoming a father, first to Ishmael, then to Isaac and the descendants, God promised him.

Notice the emotional charge in the earlier questions. Decision design looks to acknowledge emotions and use them as part of the process rather than the impossible advice of "keeping your emotions out of it." We make decisions based on what we care about; therefore, the process of decision-making cannot be emotionless, as we shall see. The state you are in when you create your vision and the feelings it evokes when you think about it are also critical parts of what makes for a compelling vision. Emotion, therefore, is an essential consideration.

Positive and negative emotional attractors

"Emotional attractor" is the term used to describe the observable characteristics of how a person thinks, including emotional, physiological, psychological, and even neurological factors.[11] Emotional attractors, positive (PEA) and negative (NEA), are states of thinking, feeling, and behaving and, as such, have an automated quality. When you are in a positive space, you will stay in a positive space until something knocks you out of that orbit. The same applies if you are in a negative spiral. This is how things will work in general. There are a couple of important notes to make. First, negative emotions are more potent than positive ones[12], and the second is related to it—life has peaks and valleys, so while you will tend to stay in whatever state you are in, the PEA will gradually decline toward the NEA. On the other hand, because negative emotions are more powerful, you need robust emotional inputs or a steady stream to supply enough of a jolt to go from NEA to PEA.

This means that positive emotions are relevant to articulating a compelling vision. These include higher levels of optimism about the future, a feeling that tomorrow will be better than today, hope and openness to possibility. Positive emotional states like these increase the likelihood of many helpful behaviours, among them improved decision-making. [13]

While positive emotion is necessary for the PEA, that is only the psycho-emotional part. Those emotions must parallel the arousal of the parasympathetic nervous system (PNS) and activation of specific areas in the brain. The PNS is the rest and digest part of the autonomic nervous system supporting the immune, neuroendocrine, and cardiovascular systems. It releases several hormones whose functions are associated with general well-being when it is active. [14]

On the other hand, you can recognise the NEA by negative

emotions such as fear, anxiety, sadness, anger, disgust, despair, and the activity of the sympathetic nervous system (SNS). The SNS is the fight or flight branch of the autonomic nervous system. As the system responsible for getting you out of troublesome situations, the SNS is active when you feel you are in physical danger, when something is important, uncertain, or when you are under pressure.[15] A vital part of the SNS is that it can be aroused merely by thinking about these. As he worried about his reception, Moses' first response to God's call was to go into NEA. He thought himself into that state. Sarah was in that state too when she thought about the possibility of bearing a child, so she laughed at the Lord's pronouncement. The things you think about can induce a psychophysiological state akin to when we are in real danger. You can spend extended periods in fight or flight mode; this is detrimental to our health and well-being.[16] Prolonged periods of negative emotion and SNS arousal can be harmful. Importantly for decision-making, long-term activation of the SNS has been found to suppress our ability to engage in effective communication due to limiting facial expression, eye gaze, hand gesture, and listening abilities.[17]

The idea is that creating a vision that will drive you, draw you and draw out of you what God specifically endowed you with takes a bit of thought. Whatever version you produce, the guarantee is that if it carries any sense of obligation, it will not get you where you want to go. It is like serving two masters, and if you coast through life, you will find yourself a servant to an expert manipulator. Saul's vision for Jonathan would have had him learning royal etiquette, distributing land, collecting taxes, and deciding where the people might have come with troubles. All of this would not only have been proper; it would have been the expectation. It would also have been unpleasant for him. He would have performed his duties but without passion or excitement. He would not have looked forward to any part of it. Living and working under these conditions arouse the SNS and observably decrease openness to innovative ideas. Suppose you have worked in something you are not passionate about (an environment that fosters the NEA state) and must subject yourself to performance reviews (another NEA stimulator). In that case, you know the struggle of low performance or being a high performer but unhappy and unfulfilled.

This brief foray into science explains the reasons behind some of the most straightforward and most powerful commands.

"Be anxious for nothing, but in everything by prayer and supplication, with thanksgiving, let your requests be made known to God." (Philippians 4:6)

"In the world, you will have tribulation; but be of good cheer, I have overcome the world." (John 16:33)

"Be strong and of good courage; do not be afraid, nor be dismayed, for the LORD your God is with you wherever you go." (Joshua 1:9)

Each is a command to shift from negative to positive, from prevention to promotion and from NEA to PEA. This chapter has been about crafting an emotionally positive and uplifting vision based on what God put inside you. The rest of the book focuses on how you can design decisions that will help you get closer to that vision. These concepts will be revisited and reinforced because, without a vision, the people perish (Proverbs 29:18). But once the vision is cast, choose you this day is the constant call. (Joshua 24:15)

3

COMMITMENT TO THE CALL

N ow the LORD had said to Abram: "Get out of your country, from your family and from your father's house to a land that I will show you. I will make you a great nation; I will bless you and make your name great, and you shall be a blessing. I will bless those who bless you, and I will curse him who curses you, and in you, all the families of the earth shall be blessed." (Genesis 12:1-3)

The Entrance of the Word

Nowhere in Scripture does God speak merely for entertainment. Whenever He speaks, it is about action, movement, and change. His word is an emissary that cannot fail in its mission. What was the impact of God calling Abram? What did it mean for God's word to come into his life? And what will it mean for you? The lessons from the scene in the region of the Gadarenes offer some answers. (Mark 5:1-20)

We can gather from Luke's record that the region included some open country for the pasturing of livestock. The community shared many things, and they were often in consensus about goings-on. When two of their own fell prey to the darkness, possessed by a legion of demons, they left them in the tombs. Perhaps they had sought the religious leaders who had prayed, attempted exorcisms, etc. Chances are someone, friends, family, or colleagues had tried to be there for them, giving them clothes, food, and shelter. Maybe there were people somewhere who held out hope that they would be healed, set free, and restored one day. Time passed, and their situation, if anything, got worse. Naturally, the country's people feared for their lives and property. And perhaps for the safety of the possessed, they eventually left them to live among the dead. The townspeople even made chains and employed guards hoping that they would be safer. Their cities and towns would be safe from the reckless violence of the spirits living in them. They took steps to ensure that if by the strength of the demons, they broke their bonds, it would be far enough away from them—that the uninhabited wilderness would be closer to the tombs than the city was so all be safe. This became normal, their everyday reality. They knew if they heard a particular sound that made your hair stand on end, it was "just Legion." It would soon pass. They knew this route would allow you to get from one place to another without meeting the demon-possessed man. They knew which area of the wilderness the spirits took him. The shepherds continued to take their flocks out to graze and drink, avoiding those areas. Business continued; boats travelled with goods and passengers, and fishers plied their trade.

It was into this scene that the Word of God stepped out. His very presence stirred things up. "Immediately", the demon-possessed men came out to meet Jesus. It was the demons asking Jesus that He not torment them. Knowing they could no longer stay, they pleaded with Him to send them off into the herd of pigs instead. To Jesus, those two were not the same. To them, human life and animal life were the same. When God created humanity, He gave him dominion over all the earth and commanded him to subdue it, including every living thing. Here in the Gadarenes, things were not as God intended. With a word that opened our eyes to that, Jesus cast out the demons, restoring health and strength to the body and to the mind soundness, serenity, and intelligence.

I imagine it was shocking to look at faces that were haunting and haunted, naked skin, mutilated, starved and skinny, and see it all reversed, healthy and whole. It was probably a little frightening to try and imagine what greatness of power had lived in them for so long. How terrible and greater still the power that had brought on this kind of change. The air of violence was gone. The men were approachable. They smiled and spoke with pleasantness in their voices, even kindness. There were witnesses to all of this, and their word spread through the region.

Having Heard the Word

"Then the whole multitude of the surrounding region of the Gadarenes asked Him to depart from them, for they were seized with great fear." (Luke 8: 37)

Unexpected. Surprising. Those are some of the words that would describe the people's response from the area. Yet, within a minute or so, we realize this is normal. It is standard in the context of decision-making.

The entrance of the Word of God into their region did not allow them to be indifferent. By freeing the demon-possessed men, Jesus was rewriting the description of the city. He exposed them to their priorities, gave them a glimpse into a new normal, a different future and asked them to consider it. They would have to redefine their culture. Some jobs, careers and titles would have to go. Some businesses would have to close. Identities would be changed, new ones assumed, and old ones abandoned. If Jesus were to stay—if the Word of God were to take root and carry out the purpose for which it (He) was sent—in the region, some doors would have to be closed while others remained open. He would cast doubt and shadow over the claims and authority of some. He would highlight the value in things, people, and places thought worthless before. Jesus' stepping off that boat was a dream for some and a nightmare for others. He was at the same time the long-awaited Messiah and a disturber of the peace.

By His very presence, Jesus showed them what He only said to others: a servant cannot serve two masters. What happened with this multitude in this region is the same thing that happened to Abram when God spoke to him. In what ways and in which areas of life did the entrance of the word of God stir things up? Where would he have to make some changes? If he was to answer that call and come to receive those promises, where would he have to leave some things behind? God's commandment was not just about the physical land. He wanted Abram to abandon some identities, titles, and entitlements. Friends, people he was in business with, plans—he had to leave them all. For His own reasons, God chose the land of the Canaanites to be the inheritance for His people. He could have chosen any country, anywhere. He also could have made Abram a blessing right where he was. The move was necessary as a measure of Abram's commitment.

Since not all significant decisions require physically uprooting everything, we can adapt the principle for our purposes. The important thing is the conviction, which feeds the commitment to those decisions. In most cases, when you must make decisions, you have a gut feeling about which way you want to go. Intuition is a natural part of everyday life, and the task is to understand why you feel that way is the right way to go. Until then, consider this approach: if you do not think it is an absolute yes, consider it a no. If you do not feel constrained and compelled to do it, in the same way that the love of Christ compels us, then pass on it, however attractive the opportunity.

4

IS THIS WHAT YOU PROMISED ME

"**N**ow there was a famine in the land, and Abram went down to Egypt to dwell there, for the famine was severe in the land" (Genesis 12:10).

A decision is a choice between at least two options, none of which are provably better or righter than the other.1 It is worth expounding on this because once we have an operational definition of what is going on, our options become more apparent. Recall the practice of changing questions from the yes and no realm to how and what. Beyond that, understanding why neither choice is more provably right than the other is helpful, not just in making the decision but in evaluating it after its implementation. The key is in the word "provably." To do so starts with taking a position and going through testing a hypothesis.

The first step is realizing that there are no facts apart from a set of specified criteria. Unless and until we agree on the conditions, however firmly and dearly, what we hold are opinions, not facts. Opinions are themselves statements or beliefs based on how someone sees something. It is merely a perspective, though that does not make it less significant.

Conditions

There is no doubt, for example, that Joseph's brothers threw him into the pit and sold him to the traders out of envy, jealousy and anger. The dreamer was clearly their father's favourite, and they couldn't stand to hear another of his self-important stories. It was an act of vengeance, of evil. There is also no doubt it was God who took Joseph from his father's land to Egypt, sending him ahead so he could save thousands of families. (Genesis 45:7) Joseph's journey was divinely designed. God orchestrated every stage. Which of these are facts? They are both versions of the same events.

What colour is the sky? And what colour is the ocean? No astronaut has ever reported crossing a blue barrier as they flew into space. Yet, from there, the seas are undeniably blue. When you step into the water, it is not some coloured substance but a clear liquid. The difference between these two facts is the conditions they are experienced. We want to ask what we need to look at, study, and test to prove this opinion a worthy consideration? In other words, what would need to be a fact to make this opinion tenable?

Think through the situation as Abram would have seen it. In obedience to a strange and formless God (relative to the gods of his fathers), he has left Mesopotamia. His father, Terah, died along the way. He did it because he believed the Lord called him to a better land, one in which he would have some position (Genesis 12:1-3. Everything God had promised was in this land. It is unclear how convincing he had had to be—his father for sure, his wife perhaps, friends, relatives and business partners. Many would have tried to convince him to stay.

Nobody moves to somewhere new expecting it to be worse than what they were leaving behind. Abram had livestock, so a place where they could graze and drink would have been the least of his expectations. If he was leaving idolatry behind, perhaps the land God showed him was full of people who worshipped Him. If not full, then at least some people so that the ridicule he had to overcome at the start of his journey would not be there. When he arrived there, "The Caananite was then in the land" and "There was a famine in the land." (Genesis 12:6, 10)

Nothing there looked like what God had promised him. In moments like that, doubt announces itself. Did you really hear from God? Was it worth leaving everything behind for this? Can you trust God to do what He said? What are you going to do now? If you take a moment to think about it, you have been in an analogous situation before. You will remember how questions such as these plagued your mind. They contaminated your vision and decision-making ability. Your problem may not have been as drastic as Abram's, but you had to commit to action. Do I stay in Canaan and wait for this famine to end? Do I go back to Mesopotamia or go to Egypt?

The famine would have pressed him to make a decision. Whether it was in the form of reports from his herders that there was little food for the animals, from his own dwindling supplies that he was unable to replenish or the caravans of people who were themselves travelling to find sustenance elsewhere, Abram needed to decide how he was going to survive the famine. Yet, this decision was about more than just the climate.

The critical issue is not too different from the one the serpent brought up with Eve. "Did God really say...? (Genesis 3:1) It is a poignant question: Are you sure that what you think you heard came from God? (Can you trust yourself?) More importantly, can you trust Him? It was He who told Him to go somewhere else. It was God who had promised to bless Abram. Going somewhere just because He said so only to find a famine is not the affirmative evidence you would expect. If you were doing okay where you were, and on His command, you find yourself in a famine with many souls looking to you for guidance and leadership—it is not a good look. Is God trustworthy?

It is easy to say yes in response because you know the Bible says so. Yet, your life and how you express your values may be saying something different. When you are having panic attacks over your family's safety on the roads, are you showing your trust in God's ability to protect you and them? When you are stressing out about being able to pay your bills and not fall further into debt, are you showing you trust Him to take care of your needs? When you cannot sleep because your mind constantly runs away with all sorts of what-if scenarios, are you bringing your cares to Him and leaving them there? Or do you go ahead as if the only correct outcome is what you envision? That says you do not trust God to fix things satisfactorily. When you cannot forgive, are you showing yourself to be a better judge than He is? Or is your decision to hold on to hurts until someone else apologizes and hoping something terrible happens, so the person pays for what they did a better form of justice than God's? Have you so convinced yourself on any matter that you have no patience, grace or compassion for others who might have different views?

Givens

Good decision-makers make a few decisions at the highest conceptual level. You need to decide on a few things that are true regardless of the situation. These are the givens of life. To use consistent language—these are the facts. As a believer, God's character ought to be a given. "Ascribe greatness to our God. He is the Rock. His work is perfect. "For all His ways are justice, a God of truth and without injustice; righteous and upright is He." (Deuteronomy 32:3-4). Abram had to believe in God's goodness, in His sovereignty, and that He is a rewarder of those who diligently seek Him. (Hebrews 11:6)

Your perspective on anything in life depends on your givens, on those things you take as your fact. If God is good, trustworthy and sovereign, then the famine in Canaan was not a failure on His part. It was not an indicator that God had abandoned Abram, nor did it say God cannot do according to His promise. The famine was not a surprise to God, something unforeseen, a wrench in His plans. To ascribe sovereignty to God is to believe He called Abram at the exact right moment so that the famine would be happening as they travelled through Canaan. The Bible says all things in creation were made by Him, for Him, and it all answers to Him. (Hebrews 11:6) That, too, was at His command. Everything then, from Abram's travel to the conditions in Canaan and the people who were there, was at God's express command or His permissive will. He could have stopped or changed it, but it happened the way it did because He chose not to. That in itself means there is no happenstance and no accidents. God intended for it to be that way.

Another given from the Bible is: "All things work together for good to those who love God, to those who are the called according to His purpose." (Romans 8:28) If God meant for Abram to be in Canaan at the time of the famine, somehow, somehow, He was going to work it out for his good. Only because Abram believes these things does he chooses not to wait out the famine or go back to Mesopotamia but to go on to Egypt. His faith in God and conviction that He would be faithful to His promise were his supports as he went further south, deeper into the unknown, farther into the uncharted.

You must make up your mind what your givens are. You do that by figuring out what you must look at, study and test (LAST). The things that LAST, that have stood the test of time, and that are reliably true no matter the circumstance need to be determined ahead of any decision. Some, you can work out ahead of time. We have already looked at the character of God. Let's consider His prescription for relationships: "Love your neighbour as yourself." (Leviticus 19:18) The true meaning of this is often underlined by what Daniel Kahneman calls WASYATI.[2] The term describes how the automatic work of the brain to make sense of the world by taking the easy route. Whatever is easily accessible to the brain, whatever takes the least effort to compute—What You See Is All There Is.

Abram believes God is good and He is trustworthy. This helps him not assume God is out to get him and that God was somehow punishing him because what he saw was not what he was expecting. Using the same approach with others is beneficial. Except for the rare sinister person, all the people you deal with are experiencing life just as you are. They have good days and bad days. They are under pressure, stressed and exhausted, just as you are. Challenges, struggles, and hurts turn up unannounced and unsolicited, just as they do for you. It is easier to see and react to an obnoxious person assume they are selfish and egotistical. When you are slighted or hurt is laborious for a brain accustomed to taking things at face value.

When you are a little less patient than usual, when the frustration from some area of your life leaks into your tone, so you sound harsh, even to people you don't know, how do you want them to treat you? Is it not with understanding, grace and forgiveness? This, then, is how you ought to treat everyone else. Jesus put an exclamation on this through the parable He taught when His audience challenged Him. He met "Who is my neighbour?" with the story of the Samaritan. (Luke 10:30-37) Through it, He said to show forgiveness, kindness, and grace to the one you wouldn't usually have dealings with. For those people, He said go to great lengths, meet their needs, accommodate them, help them to the point of undue hardship—the Samaritan put the robbery victim on his own beast while he walked. Who knows how far it was to the inn? And once there, he paid out of pocket and promised to cover any additional costs incurred while he was gone. All for a stranger from among people who hated everything he was and stood for.

This is impossible if you take things at face value. If you allow the preferences and prejudices you have always lived with to dictate your behaviour, you will find it hard to walk out the command, "Love your neighbour as yourself." On the other hand, if you are aware of how you will express your value, commit to loving your neighbour, and treat others as you would have them treat you (Matthew 7:12), then your behaviour is not determined by the particulars of each moment. You are not reactive. You are not at the mercy of whoever and whatever you encounter.

Reputation

Whether in business or relationships, the Bible teaches (It's a given that whatever is in the book is true!) there is nothing new under the sun. (Ecclesiastes 1:9) Because of that, it's a little easier to make your decisions ahead of time. The conundrum you face in every moment of decision is not new. Others had to make the same decision before, which means you can learn from them. With a bit of study, you can find out how they came to choose one way or the other and how things turned out. If there is a lousy outcome every time someone gets into a partnership with another whose reputation raises questions, there is a fact you don't need to re-establish: bad company corrupts good morals. You cannot make a good deal with a bad person. "It's better to hang out with people better than you. Pick out associates whose behaviour is better than yours and you'll drift in that direction." [3] All of this puts a premium on the character of the people we keep close. Therefore, you can choose ahead of time the things that matter most will involve only those preceded by a reputation of integrity, honesty, compassion and whatever else you may value. Then, as you live your life, resist any opportunity or offer, no matter how lucrative or beneficial, if the others do not pass that test of character.

The givens in your life, the facts you hold to be accurate, determine the lens through which you see things. They are the key to what you see and why you see things the way you do. They are the framework for your perspective—and your perspective matters.

5

THAT I MAY LIVE BECAUSE OF YOU

And it came to pass, when he was close to entering Egypt, that he said to Sarai his wife, "Indeed, I know that you are a woman of beautiful countenance. Therefore it will happen, when the Egyptians see you, that they will say, 'This is his wife,' and they will kill me, but they will let you live. Please say you are my sister, that it may be well with me for your sake, and that I may live because of you." (Genesis 12:11-13)

Your perspective matters so much that, like your reputation, you must guard it. This is not referring to your opinion as much as how you *choose* to look at things. Curiosity is a perspective. Optimism, faith, and hope are too. It is an attitude; a way of being. One that does not shift, or change based on the circumstances.

Abram's perspective was God is trustworthy and wherever He led, Abram would go. When he made this decision, we will never know but it was at some point before the story in the Bible begins. It had to be so as Abram was untroubled when a God who was a stranger to him and his fathers called him to leave his country. He travelled the land, believed when the promise was confirmed and offered sacrifices as proof of that. The severe famine simply moved him further south where he hoped to find sustenance, but he remained unmoved in his faith.

The first recording of Abram speaking in this saga shows us a different side of the man. Simply put, Abram was afraid. As he thought about his life in the culture he lived in, Abram held on to his belief that God could move in his life with all power, but in the finer matters, Abram would have to fend for himself. He spoke so matter-of-factly ("they will say...they will kill me") that we are forced to believe what he predicted was a picture of what happened in his days. To secure a beautiful woman, men in power often (if not always) killed her husband if she was married, but treated any man who looked after her, like a brother or father. Whatever the case, Abram's faith in what God was able to do did not extend to keeping him alive in Egypt.

Abram asked his wife to tell a half-truth, to work on a technicality. She was his sister, but their parentage was far enough that they could marry. It was like an inside joke; they could both pass a polygraph if it came to that, and it gave them some temporary respite when thinking about what could happen. How often do you make choices that give you short-term rest, satisfaction, or peace? How often do you make decisions that make you feel better in the moment, but don't really solve the issue at hand?

Asking these questions is another aspect of good decision-making. Think of it as time travel: could you live for the next ten years with the state of things your decision sets up? This is the same question people are getting at when they say, what advice would your 80-year-old self give to you? Some of the most innovative companies have developed a similar habit. Before a decision is executed, experts in whatever field are called and asked a peculiar question: Fastforward a year or two from now. Imagine that this project failed. What went wrong? This is a process known as a *premortem* or prospective hindsight.[1] Research shows imagining an event has already occurred increases the ability to correctly identify reasons for future outcomes by thirty percent and helps name possible risks at the outset.[2]

Abram's way out of a tight spot put Sarai in an awkward position. Abram's wife was a beautiful, public, and obvious blessing so that at 65 years old, men were looking at Sarai and commending her to Pharaoh. Her beauty was such that she was taken to him right away. While telling everybody Abram was her brother kept him, Abram, alive, she was whisked off to the palace and prepared to be among the monarch's wives. What happens when Pharaoh wants to consummate the marriage? What happens when he wants to take her into his bed, free of guilt because he had done the thing properly? Not only was Abram kept alive, but Pharaoh also treated him well for Sarai's sake. He was comfortable; she was edgy. He could be thinking, not only can they survive the severe famine in Egypt, but they can also wait it out on the royal dime. In the meantime, she was incredibly anxious. How long will she have to invent excuses for not sleeping with her new husband? What happens when she runs out of stories? Will she just give in and sleep with him, or will the weight of the lie overcome her? And if she told the truth, how would Pharaoh react? He would not appreciate the deception, that was for sure. To what extent would he go to express his displeasure? Would she be executed, beaten, or imprisoned? What would Abram's fate be?

Making good decisions is hard at the best of times. Making them under stress is that much more challenging. Unless you know ahead of time you will be under some sort of pressure and you prepare accordingly, it is almost impossible to make choices that do not open the door for regret in the near future. Fear, and its close cousins anxiety, worry and anger have the uncanny ability to befuddle the best brains. The most intelligent and the faithful behave in foolish and faithless ways under their influence.

Emotions: A Legitimate and Important Part of Decision-Making

There is no brain centre for decision-making or emotion. Rather, there are patterns of activity in the brain that, if we know how to recognize them, we can identify certain themes and guess what someone might be feeling or experiencing, especially during decision-making. Of course, this is if you had fancy machines and you could do some functional magnetic resonance imaging or fMRIs.

Those who have them have made interesting discoveries. Neuroscientists have mapped out the neural patterns associated with emotions, and they have some recognizable physiological markers.[3] Fear, anger, love, and anxiety, just to name a representative few, are all associated with and trigger the sympathetic nervous system. Because of that, we can recognize the classic symptoms of increased heart rate and heightened focus. Blood pressure tends to go up. Blood is shunted more toward the larger muscle groups in anticipation of the need to fight or flee in situations where danger might be clear/approaching. This is also true if the situation calls for connecting, making friends—anything that is important and worth bringing focused attention to. So what we experience as feelings are neurological and physiological patterns as the brain gives meaning to the data it is receiving. They affect what we think of people, our appraisal of our environments, what we take in and what we leave out. We feel our way through life, and our thoughts catch up with how we feel. You know this to be true if you have ever felt you could trust people or got a certain 'vibe' about them even if you do not even know their names. Seldom do you change your opinion about someone after you have had that vibe. All of this shows emotions play a role in the decision-making process.

Emotions are rich reserves of information.[4] If you look at them appropriately, they will tell you what is important to you, what you are passionate about and what you value. In this way, they point you in the right direction. At other times, however, they can get you into trouble. When emotions simply "flood" your brain, you can be completely unaware of anything else. (This is what we are saying when we say, "love is blind!")

You could say that blindness was involved in the pact between Abram and Sarai. The biggest indicator of this is that Abram says if he is to live in Egypt, it would be up to what she does. When we read the story, it seems Abram is a "grown-up believer" because he made an unthinkable move the first time he was called. This request says he had some growing to do too. To think his life was in the hands of someone who is just as fallible, just as prone to hurts, injuries and doubts, someone who depended on *him*, is because something was blinding him to a truth that is fundamental to being a believer. That thing was fear, and the truth it obscured was the sovereignty of God.

What Abram and Sarai needed to remember was that life begins and ends with God. He is involved in every second, every moment in between. His Lordship, influence and preeminence are over all people, cultures, and countries. In one word, control. God is in control and perhaps it is that part of His image that He has put in us, but we all desire to have a measure of control over our lives. Some like to have tight control over every aspect of their lives. For others, if they have the say in a few areas, they are happy to let others direct some sections of their lives.

"O LORD, I know the way of man is not in himself. It is not in man who walks to direct his own steps." (Jeremiah 10:23)

"Or do you not know that your body is the temple of the Holy Spirit who is in you, whom you have from God, and you are not your own? For you were bought at a price; therefore glorify God in your body and in your spirit, which are God's." (1 Corinthians 6:19-20)

The words of both the Old and the New Testament make it clear to be a follower of Christ, however, is to cede control. It is not just accepting this but finding comfort, safety and hope in it. It is to *prefer* having Him in charge. Do you find it easy to trust God's way of providing for your family? Are you content not knowing what plans He has for your future? Do you have confidence your children will be safe when you leave them in His hands? If you have trouble with any of these, you are in company with Abram. It is possible to trust God with your eternal destiny and still want to control how the here and now go.

"That I may live because of you" does not look like a control issue at face value, but control issues never do. By putting it in Sarai's hands, Abram wants to put his life in a place he can influence. And by scripting Sarai's conversation points once they get to Egypt, he is hoping to extend how much say he has on what will happen to him.

We started this chapter by discussing the importance of perspective. If you, like Abram, look around and see the realities of your culture, you will be overcome by the events and stories that are commonplace where you are. For most people, events and stories are facts, and they operate as if they are. This, of course, does not hold up to a little injection of logic. The words Abram uses (they will say... they will kill) make those things definitive. He leaves us in no doubt, begging the question, why *didn't he* have any doubt? What made him so sure? Chances are, he had heard a story where something similar happened. Even less likely is it happened to somebody he knew. It just so happened that it went exactly as he described. Overconfidence is one of the conditions that precipitate poor decisions.

Heuristics in decision-making

First, there is the assumption that since it happened to somebody, and I heard about it, it must happen a lot. With social media and innumerable news outlets, the same news headline can dominate what we see, read, and hear about for a long time. Somehow, our antennas are trained to look for and respond to negative news. The videos about cute babies and animals, acts of kindness and courage, if they make the news at all, are squeezed into the last few minutes of the news segment. The rest is dominated by violence, deception, corruption and blame games. Significantly more articles covering accidents, murder, robbery, and other expressions of evil circulate than do those of the opposite, more positive stories. All of this makes us think those things are far more prevalent than they are. In fact, Steven Pinker showed through his research that the world is much safer now than it used to be, and the trend has been that way for some time.[5] It is only that, with camera phones, blogs, options to "like," comment and share virtually everything on the internet, there is far more coverage of the same stuff, making it seem as if there is more of it. Believing something bad could be just around the corner, it is logical that you would take precautions. That is exactly what Abram did. This logic, however, is based on a little trick your brain plays on you.

We all know there are more people in the world than our immediate circle. All the people we *do not* talk to at the grocery store prove that to us every day. Yet, how often have you made inferences about how the rest of your town or city is doing based on the experiences that are common to you and your circle? It is mind-blowing how the winners of the Major League Baseball tournament every year are called "world champions." How can that be when the sport only has American teams playing (and one from Canada)? Or the countless times it has been said, "The world is watching." This is clearly not true because we know for certain there are people in the world who do not have televisions. And among those that do, there are many who are asleep, at work or simply not interested in whatever the event is that the entire world is supposedly watching. Statements like these come from thinking the behaviour (or beliefs) of a small group reflects the population at large. If you check anything in a small sample size, you will get skewed results.[6]

Third, the brain does not like being wrong. You are familiar with that feeling of, "Why did I even try?" and the awkwardness, embarrassment, shame and the "I'm never doing that again" type of thinking that goes with not getting something right. The urge to save face (even when no one is looking) is linked to self-esteem, and nobody wants to sit by while this or that cracks the wall of his/her self-image. So when it comes to answering questions and creating a narrative about the world, the brain does several things. When asked a question that is too difficult to answer, or one that will spend too much of the brain's bandwidth, it simply substitutes it with an easier question and answers that one. God called us to move and when we did, we came to a land where there was a famine. Now I am forced into Egypt. Can I trust Him? That is a hard question. So the brain might circumvent the first question and answer, what can I do to keep myself safe in this situation?

The substitution happens so quickly, you do not even notice it and if you do not put in the work to make sure you are answering the right questions, you will set yourself up to make poor decisions repeatedly. Therefore the pre-decision work of deciding on your values and deciding on the facts is so helpful. Equally important, is writing down the decision you are trying to make. When you change your questions and prove what the facts are, you create the very conditions that make thinking even more of an energy-consuming task. It makes things harder and when things get difficult substitution is the preferred choice for your brain.

Another trick the brain uses to avoid everything associated with being wrong is that it sifts the world looking for things that confirm what it already believes. This is known as confirmation bias. Think of how social media works. Each platform is run by an algorithm that *learns*. So when you "like" something, it gives you more of that. Where it used to be a little subtle, there are many options now to choose the news channel you want, artists, sports bulletins, etc. You can curate your world to reflect only who you like and what you agree with while cancelling, cutting or otherwise ignoring what you do not. It is no wonder when it comes to information, the most well-read today is simply well informed about stuff they already know. They have read and heard the same ideas, opinions, and sentiments from many diverse sources. For Abram, the effects of these are clear later in the story. God intervened in Egypt, but not before things had gone exactly as Abram said they would. The Egyptians *did* find Sarai beautiful; they *did* commend her to Pharaoh, and he did take her for himself. Having said Abram was her brother, Pharaoh did treat him well for her sake. All this only served to confirm to Abram he was right about what to expect. That made him feel his decision was justified so much that he used the same strategy when he met Abimelech for the first time.

Often, poor choices are rewarded with good outcomes and learning opportunities are lost. Abram's dishonesty was not punished; though God intervenes nothing is said to reprimand this type of behaviour. Things work out despite poor or no planning in most of life and you do not really learn how much time and effort go into making things turn out the way you want. Luck plays a much greater role than we would care to acknowledge—like the time you made it to your appointment despite leaving home late. You had no say in what colour the lights along the way would be and if two or three of them were a different colour when you arrived, or there was an accident, your lateness might have had different consequences. Just because you have not been caught speeding, it does not mean speeding is a clever idea. Yet, because your behaviour has not been reprimanded, you do it once and again. So the next time you plan poorly, sleep through your alarm or just do not think to give yourself a buffer between appointments, your operating system is thinking about all the times you drove above the speed limit and made it. If I did it then, you think, I can do it now. If it worked then it will work now. That is confirmation bias and the planning fallacy at work.

When you assume events and stories are facts when you act without giving the law of small numbers the attention it deserves when you do not realize the question, you are paying attention to is the substitute question from the one you started with, you are prone to plan without seeing the bigger picture. Each of these is happening all the time. When they are combined, stirred together in a pot of stress and fear, as with Abram, bad decisions can be expected. What we are discussing here is decision design. It is about knowing what makes a decision good, and how you can make more of them.

6

CONFLICT RESOLUTION

Earlier, I noted Abram's partial obedience to the command to leave his father's family behind. Lot is the one who benefits from this expression of familial obligation on Abraham's part. This interaction between them set the stage for a few concepts to frame the whole idea of decision design.

Relationships, Health and Money

On the other side of the goings-on in Egypt, we read: "So Abram said to Lot, "Please let there be no strife between you and me, and between my herdsmen and your herdsmen; for we are brethren. Is not the whole land before you? Please separate from me. If you take the left, then I will go to the right; or, if you go to the right, then I will go to the left" (Genesis 13:8-9).

When it comes to sin, the author of the book of Hebrews says, "Therefore we also, since we are surrounded by so great a cloud of witnesses, let us lay aside every weight, and the sin which so easily ensnares us, and let us run with endurance the race that is set before us." (Hebrews 12:1) There may be many weights, but there is *the* sin- just one. There are many faces regarding decision-making, but the actual issues within those decisions are few. Every decision you make is about relationships, money, or health. The three are intertwined, so any decision you need to make likely involves all three, with different situations changing the weight of each category. If you investigate it, these same categories have been offered before, with other titles.

Take, for example, the three temptations Jesus suffered in the desert (Luke 4:1-14). The Devil came to Him after He was fasting for forty days and immediately spoke about food. Then he challenges Jesus to prove His relationship to the Father by jumping off the top of the temple. When Jesus stood firm on those, the Devil offered Him the world and its glory. The enemy passed health, relationship, and money before Him. The question of Jesus being the Son of God was pivotal to each, suggesting that relationship is the most critical of the three. This aligns with God's declaration that it is not good for man to be alone at the beginning of time. (Genesis 13:10) When asked about the most important commandments, Jesus focused their attention on the quality of their relationship, quality defined by love. "Love the Lord your God with all your heart, with all your soul, and with all your strength," and "love your neighbour as yourself." (Matthew 22:37-39) When the prophets summarized the requirements, they said, love mercy, do justice and walk humbly with your God—relationships. (Micah 6:8)

The conflict that arose between Abram's herdsmen and those of his nephew was a matter of presenting to their masters fatted calves and sheep. Abram and Lot hired them to do a job, and the fighting between them showed the loyalty each group had to its master. What they could produce directly influenced their employer's financial standing. Abram, taking in the bigger picture, recognized that neither his nephew nor his herders were the problem. As such, he did not attack them but focused on finding a solution targeted at the real issue—the land. God blessed them so much that the land could not bear to have them so close to each other. Each needed a bit more elbow room. Abram got them both what they needed, and he did it in a way that ensured their relationship remained intact.

The significance of Abram's approach is most apparent when you consider how they got to that point. Abram took Lot in after Haram's death. He took Lot with him when he moved from Mesopotamia. It would be reasonable to continue as if Abram had taught Lot everything he knew, being the father figure. Lot would have benefited from his wisdom, as well as his blessings. When the altercation happened, Abram could have pulled rank. He could have pointed out all the above and told Lot where to go. Instead of taking an aggressive stance and drawing a line in the sand, Abram takes a more pleading approach.

Please separate from me. If you take the left, then I will go to the right; or, if you go to the right, then I will go to the left. And Lot lifted his eyes and saw all the plain of Jordan, that it was well watered everywhere (before the LORD destroyed Sodom and Gomorrah) like the garden of the LORD, like the land of Egypt as you go toward Zoar. Then Lot chose for himself all the plain of Jordan, and Lot journeyed east. And they separated from each other. (Genesis 13:9-11)

Abram shows the height of faith and love—giving without conditions in the service of a relationship. He did not investigate the land and offer Lot the choice he did not want. He was happy to take whatever Lot *did not* want if they could stay connected.

Many people have condemned Lot for his choice but unfairly so. Consider this: the separation was not due to a disagreement between Abram and Lot but between their herders. What could they be possibly fighting over but water supply and pasture? With this as a basis for the argument and the "whole land" before him, it makes sense that Lot would make the decision based on what was scarce and fueling the conflict.

Jordan was well watered everywhere, not too long after

the severe famine that had seen them all go down to Egypt. Moreover, it was like the garden of the LORD. (Genesis 13:10) Wouldn't *you* want to live in that land, especially if you had flocks and herds?

The righteousness or wickedness of the people had no part to play in his decision. When Abram and his party came into Canaan, they were inhabitants of the land. The final word on Lot—getting drunk and fathering his daughters' children—is less than stellar. But the two men were more alike than they were different: Abram jumped to his feet to minister to the angels, pleading with them to stop for a while to rest. He made them some food, and they went on their way. So did Lot. The LORD's evaluation was that Lot was righteous, and He gave Lot a chance to get out of the city before destroying it (Genesis 19). It is unfounded to assume that the way of life of the citizens of those cities was what attracted him. The Bible says he was looking for land that would be conducive to raising flocks.

This is what makes Abram's approach to peacemaking even more remarkable. Everything Lot went through, Abram was right there beside him. He, too, had flocks and herds and had suffered the famine. That means Abram had the exact needs, and what would have offered a reprieve to Lot would have done the same for him. So Abram was aware of the plain of Jordan just as well. The LORD had spoken the promise to *him*, Abram. He could have told Lot where to go and chosen Jordan or any other part of the land for himself. Instead, he laid it all out.

We are often taken in by the circumstances around the question/decision and think there is little time to think things through. As a result, we make many decisions prematurely. Now consider that many things simply sort themselves without any intervention. When faced with an apparent fork in the road, we seldom ask what happens if I do *nothing*? It will not apply to every decision you have to make, just as it would not have been a possibility between Abram and Lot. Their herders would have just continued to fight, with the whole thing possibly becoming messier. It is, however, a question worthy of your attention.

Humanity has a bias toward taking some action, even when there is no evidence that it would be better than doing nothing. In any given situation, because of that habit of substituting one question for another, which your brain has, you will find that when you are thinking about what you should do, your focus is already on one thing when the issue is quite another.

Compromises

Every decision you make will involve some compromise. You would be better off understanding what types of concessions you must choose than pretend there are no compromises. In so doing, you will make better decisions. These compromises depend very much on putting in the work to define the problem and what the decision must achieve to make it a good one. In other words, you need to evaluate a decision before you even make it! The bread and the baby illustrate two types of compromises.

On a night out, you will undoubtedly consider the comfort and ambience, the service, location, and the price of the meals where you are going to go. You might even think about whether the food on offer meets your definition of healthy or not—do they have vegan or gluten-free meals? All of these are key features, but this is a decision about whether to eat. When you look at it from this level, it becomes clear why you have so often said (especially if there are others to think about before making the decision), "That doesn't matter." "I'm not too worried about that," or even, "It doesn't matter; let us just get something." In other words, all of those features you think about would be great to have if possible, but the critical thing is that you eat. You are willing to compromise on some things so you can eat. In other words, half a loaf is still bread, and it is better than no bread at all.[1]

In contrast, when two women show up, each claiming to be the baby's mother (1 Kings 3:16-23), a different type of compromise is on the table. As the story goes, two women who had given birth around the same time came before King Solomon, asking him to give a ruling that would settle the matter. With each claiming it was the other who had lost a baby during the night, Solomon had one choice to break the tie. "Bring me a sword," he said. "We'll cut the living baby into two, and they can each have half." Of course, half a baby is not a baby at all but a corpse. Having gone through all three trimesters with their characteristic challenges and then given birth, no woman would say, "Cut him in half." She would rather give the baby away than see him mutilated. This is where the king made the decision, and it is where you will decide too.

For those decisions you will have to make, you will find yourself having to determine whether the compromise in front of you is the bread or the baby type. Abram valued family, and there was little, save obedience to God, that was too sacred a sacrifice to keep healthy, positive relationships with them. So when he thought about resolving the conflict, he didn't think about his rights as the older man. He didn't ruminate about whether his nephew and his herdsmen were showing him respect or not. Abram chose to give up the best of the land so that he might preserve the relationship with his nephew. He believed that God would bless him no matter what he ended up with after the two had separated. He did not need to take the best for himself or put someone else down to feel good or succeed.

Relationships are the baby type of compromise. Toxic relationships are corpses, or they will create some very quickly. When God said, "It is not good for man to be alone," He intended for the people in your life to be nourishing, building, and encouraging. You will have to talk with them and mend the relationships or separate from those who have the opposite effect. Abram created distance between himself and his nephew and thereby between the herdsmen. Most importantly, he did it in a way that kept their relationship alive.

Many deathbed scenes, whether in the movies or in real life, include regrets over time wasted in disagreements, fights, anger, and unforgiving behaviour that created strangers out of families. It may be worth the time for you and those you love to think ahead about how you want to approach conflict. Resolution can end amicably with each of you learning something about the other. A moment of being at odds can, in the future, be one of those things that contribute to how tightly knit you are to a friend or family member. Or it can end in you not speaking to each other, holding grudges. Emotions often cloud the landscape of conflict. Reminders to see the situation as the issue and the other person as a collaborator can help you refrain from saying or doing things in the heat of the moment. A commitment to hate the sin and not the sinner is Godlike, and it is to this lofty height you will want to be reaching. It is hard at the best of times. It becomes impossible when you are hurt or angry unless you set your mind to think this way before getting yourself in an altercation.

The land and resources the herders fought over were of the bread type of compromise. It is far better to own a part of the hope diamond than 100 percent of a rhinestone. This kind of thinking gave Abram the freedom to approach the situation the way he did. He could find other pastures for his livestock. The spot they were in was not the only one in all the land where animals could thrive. And with God's promise, the reason he was there in the first place, Abram could expect God would bless him no matter what he was left with after Lot made his choice.

When you make a decision, you must understand what category (relationships, finances, or health) and whether the compromise is the baby or bread type. What you do, that is, if you should do anything, should reflect these things. Each of these concepts plays a role in Abram's life in the following chapters.

7

BOUNDARIES AND COSTS

Being the son of Abram's younger brother Nahor, Lot was Abram's nephew. Yet, the Bible refers to Lot as Abram's brother, perhaps an indicator of how family members related to each other back then. It is also a mark of the enduring relationship between them. Abram's approach to sorting out the issue between the herders focused on preserving the relationship while getting them both what they wanted. He also decided, knowing there is no such thing as *one* decision. Every choice is possible because of those made before it. Each also lays the groundwork for those to come.

Abram could have taken a "This is how it's going to be" approach with no thought for the future. If he had, this passage would not be there:

"Now, when Abram heard that his brother was taken captive, he armed his three hundred and eighteen trained servants who were born in his own house and went in pursuit as far as Dan. He divided his forces against them by night, and he and his servants attacked them and pursued them as far as Hobah, which is north of Damascus. So he brought back all the goods and also brought back his brother Lot and his goods, as well as the women and the people." (Genesis 14:14-16)

Separating amicably meant Abram was still moved to action when he heard his brother was in trouble. It did not matter how significant the opposition would be. There was no hesitation, no calculation of his chances of winning the battle or whether it was even possible. Abram heard Lot was in trouble, and he got to work doing something about it.

Cost vs. Price

We cannot go ahead without spending time on one of the most basic elements of decision-making, whether you routinely consider the ideas you have learned about so far or not. Every decision has a *cost*. Friends have become enemies, regrets have been birthed and nursed, families and friendships destroyed, and businesses have gone under because of decisions made without taking the time to consider the cost beyond what is immediately apparent.

When he heard the news of Lot's capture, Abram mastered what he had at his disposal. He went to rescue his brother at the head of 318 servants. We do not know whether he knew he would be battling the armies of five kings before he went on his quest, though it does not seem as if that would have stopped him. Some of the herders who had striven with those of Lot were probably among those servants. They did not owe Lot anything. They would have had families of their own to think about. But for the cause of their master, they took up arms. Most of them would have been relatively young, with few as old as Abram was. Their courage and loyalty were plain for all to see. Yet, it must be said they followed Abram with no guarantee of success. There was no guarantee of a safe and healthy return, though they would have their share of the plunder of war, *should* they return. To save Abram's family, others placed themselves in harm's way. For Lot's sake, some young men were probably never to marry. Husbands, fathers, and sons would potentially not return.

Individual situations have different elements about them, which means you will have to calculate the relative cost of each decision. Yet, knowing the relative cost, i.e., what it might cost you, is only part of the equation. Even then, particularly for things you buy, the price is what you think of when we discuss cost. What it costs you to make that transaction *is more* than just matching the tag. It is a function of the price, the size of the stores from which you would be withdrawing that amount. It is also about how you feel about what is left, among other things. Do you feel what remains leaves you in good stead to do whatever else you may have planned? Add to this the thoughts and feelings of others who will be affected by this decision, and things get more complicated.

Decisions, therefore, are emotional things. Despite all evidence and advice, it is impossible to "remove emotions" from decision-making. Humans are emotional creatures, even those among us who believe they come to their choices "using logic." When we talk about whether a decision was worth it, we consider whether we feel our emotional account is in the black after seeing what happens. Regret is how we punish ourselves when things do not work out the way we hoped, and we can imagine the alternatives we could have taken. The fear of regret and the move to avoid it is a powerful motivator. As psychologists define it, regret is when you reflect on a decision and have feelings that you should have known better. There is a sinking feeling with thoughts about your mistakes and the opportunities lost in close attendance. There is a tendency to kick oneself an urge to correct one's mistakes, undo the event and get a second chance.[1] With all that, you can give yourself some grace for wanting to sidestep it all.

↑ Boundary conditions

One way to minimise the risk of regret, of having red in the emotional ledger, is to define the conditions a decision must satisfy. In other words, making an effective decision is not possible until you consider the various elements of the situation have and ensure the decision that follows addresses each one to an acceptable level of satisfaction.

Consider two scenarios:

> Imagine you had $3000 in the stock market. At the end of a particularly rough day, you find out your portfolio is down $36. How would do you feel? Would you feel it is time to sell?

> Imagine leading an army of 3000, and you lost the territorial battle. In the aftermath, you realise that 36 of your men lost their lives as you were forced into retreat. How would you feel? Would you feel differently if you had lost those men but won the battle?

In the first scenario, you would need to access those mental files that serve as your guidelines for how to behave financially. Investing is undoubtedly a matter of risk tolerance, and for some, this would be enough to prove that trading on the market is a risk not worth taking. For others, it would be acceptable as part of the furniture—daily fluctuations are not of concern. There are far too many variables that interact innumerably to affect the stock price. If the trend over a five- or ten-year period shows steady growth, $36 is negligible. That is a boundary condition.

In both cases, it is a loss of 0.012 percent. In the second scenario, however, human lives are the subject. How much did the outcome of the battle influence your feelings about those lives lost? Was it victory at all costs? Or was there an acceptable number of lives that could be sacrificed for the good of the cause? These would be boundary conditions.

Abram caught up to the armies of the kings and did whatever was necessary to restore Lot and all that was his without incurring any losses. They walked away with their mission accomplished and the bonus of the spoils of war. The decision to go after those armies was the right one. It was well worth it. This is a retrospective opinion, or what is also known as hindsight bias. It's that "I knew it right from the start" feeling. If you have ever heard or said, "Was there ever any doubt?" that was hindsight bias. *Because* it all worked out, what they did was the obvious idea and the only one that could have worked. It was the logical choice, the only choice.

Had things gone differently, had some of his servants died, but they had still been able to rescue Lot, it may have been a bitter-sweet victory. But it would have been a victory nonetheless because the condition that needed to be met by the decision was clear—rescue Lot from captivity. Though not explicitly said, the mission included bringing him, his wife and everything that belonged to him home alive. If the condition to meet were feeling avenged for the attack on and capture of Lot, the strategy taken would have been different. It may have included slaughtering everything in their wake, women, children, and animals. It may have sanctioned whatever action so the five kings would know the name of Abram, fear him and take care never to touch anything or anyone attached to him ever again.

Substitution and Intelligent behaviour

You can only make good decisions when you have definitively answered this question: what is this decision session to achieve? Doing so creates a slight but crucial distinction between getting things done and not. Recall the action bias—our tendency to do something simply because doing something helps with the feeling of control. It is rife among professionals in the financial sector. Banks and other trading platforms offer discounts on your account fees if you have many trades per quarter. They incentivise behaviours that benefit them since they apply a surcharge for every transaction. In stark contrast, the world's foremost investor, Warren Buffet, approaches it differently after buying stock in a business. The ideal length of time to hold that stock, his favourite time, is "forever," so long as the company generates above-average returns and management behaves rationally. "Inactivity strikes us as intelligent behaviour." [2] Granted, there are many approaches to operating in the stock market, and you must choose a style that works for you. The point remains the same- you need to clarify the objective before deciding. That way, you can be sure whether the choice you made checks off those conditions or not. If the aim is to make the banks much money while losing a lot of yours, Warren Buffet's reputation is unwarranted. If, however, you want to get a good return on your investment and see compound interest at work, then the many trades per quarter may not be the best approach. It may satisfy the feeling of doing something, but it misses the aim.

Many decisions are simply to satisfy the ego. These are the things you will see people who have just received a new title do. They will start or stop something just so those around them know they have the power to do so. Fear is another reason people make the decisions they do. Fear of getting hurt, being alone, what others may think about them, or fear that someone might find out the ugly things they think about themselves. Whatever it is, few decisions made from a place of fear are good. They might make you feel less afraid at the moment, and that momentary relief from that weight feels good. It makes you feel as if the decision was the right one. That feeling is deceptive.

The goal is not to make it so you are not scared. Nor is it to pay your ego and feel a foot taller. It certainly is not to remove your anxiety. In each of these cases, your brain has substituted the main goal for secondary options. Substitution happens so often, considering it gives more credence to the oft-given advice to write things down. Write your goals and aims down. Think through the conditions surrounding those to minimise the chances of substitution and the resultant consequences when making decisions.

Misdirected Efforts

Saul would be the poster child for this.

God handpicked him to be the first king of Israel. Though his choice was, in the Lord's eyes, a rejection of Him as king over His people, God was not going to install someone incapable just to say, "I told you so," as soon as he failed. Saul had a presence, standing head and shoulders over everyone else. He was a man of war with the Spirit of the Lord upon him; he was the right man to defend Israel from her enemies. As the oil that Samuel poured over him flowed through his hair, beard and onto his clothes, Saul learned that the LORD had anointed him commander over His inheritance. The throne over Israel was never his. It was borrowed. To keep it and see his sons inherit it, all he had to do was, "Fear the LORD and serve Him and obey His voice, and do not rebel against the commandment of the LORD." (1 Samuel 12:14) Those were the conditions his decisions had to meet, and he did it well.

In two short years, however, Saul was drunk with the corrupting influence of power. He loved the accolades, and every decision he made from then on took him further from God. By the time Goliath came into the picture, Saul had changed. He had forgotten that the LORD could still accomplish salvation in Israel. When the Philistine said, "I defy the armies of Israel this day; give me a man, that we may fight together" (1 Samuel 17:10-11), Saul and all of Israel were dismayed and afraid. That he was scared had less to do with Goliath's stature and prowess as a warrior and more to do with the growing distance between Saul and the One who chose him.

God anointed another who knew where his help came from. David killed Goliath and led Israel's armies countless times at Saul's behest. As David proved his effectiveness repeatedly, his popularity grew. The songs the people sang humiliated and infuriated Saul so much that blindness covered him, and where David may have been a way back for him, Saul spent the rest of his life trying to kill him. When the people needed him to defend his country's borders, he was absent chasing David in caves. When an evil spirit tormented him, and David was the one person who could help him through his music, Saul kept trying to pin him to the wall with his spear. Though Jonathan died with him in battle, there is no doubt Saul no longer shared the closeness he once had with his son after Saul berated him for having a friendship with David.

In the story of Saul, we find the ultimate warning against substitution and the lack of a clear set of boundary conditions to measure your decisions against. The cost of not heeding this warning is too great.

Behold, to obey is better than sacrifice, and to heed than the fat of rams. (1 Samuel 15:22)

8

RIGHT PEOPLE, RIGHT SEATS

The journey back from Lot's rescue includes an unexpected encounter. If it were a modern-day story, it would be someone saying they met an angel. Melchizedek appeared out of nowhere and was gone just as quickly. Yet, this experience had a lasting impact on Abram's life.

The old priest was the first person Abram met who believed in the same God. For both, He is the Highest, and He is everything. Something about Melchizedek convinced Abram of this. They sat down together to eat, and Melchizedek blessed Abram.

"Blessed be Abram of God Most High, Possessor of heaven and earth; and blessed be God Most High, who has delivered your enemies into your hand." (Genesis 14:20)

Melchizedek had something to say to Abram, but he could not say it apart from who God is. And for the way God blessed His servant, He was worthy of praise at the same time.

The two shared a value and a perspective. It was this that brought them to a meal together. In a discussion about decision-making, the choice of companionship deserves attention. God said it right at the start, "It is not good for man to be alone."

(Genesis 2:18) His solution was to give Adam someone compatible with him. In vision, purpose, and plan, she fulfilled Adam's needs in ways science is still proving today.

Friends and Companions

A sound support system has proven precisely what God meant to happen with good company in every discipline tested. Productivity is up, and physiological and psychological well-being are enhanced so much that the California Department of Mental Health said: "Friends can be good medicine." [1] Studies have shown a double impact on health. Elements in the body change to a more healthy-looking profile and buffer against disease. It's like building a solid foundation for a building and putting a moat around it for extra protection when stress levels are high. Researchers found this buffering effect across all ages, genders, and ethnic groups. Statistically, people who had fewer close friends were two to three times more likely to die during the study than those who had more close friends to turn to when they needed them. This was true even after adjusting for smoking and histories of major illnesses. [2]

In another five-year study, researchers observed two groups in motor skills and, staying on theme, decision-making. The key difference between the groups was how well they knew each other. One group comprised of friends, and the other, acquaintances who barely knew each other. On average, the friends completed three times more projects and were up to twenty percent more effective in their decision-making than their counterparts. [3]

Bad company, however, corrupts good morals. (1 Corinthians 15:33)

While God intended for man to be with others, His plan was not for just anyone to fill the space. The Bible says Jesus spent all night in prayer before He picked His disciples. (Mark 3:13-14) He had thousands to choose from, and He could have chosen any of them. So why did He approach it the way He did? There was a calling on Jesus' life, and He wanted those who would be closest to Him to be those who would help Him in His mission. He came to seek and save the lost. Those He chose were among the lost and, having saved them, chose them to be with Him. He let them see Him triumph and struggle. They saw Him cry and pray. They were there when the crowds accepted Him and the cities rejected Him. Jesus confided in them, and they in Him. They perplexed Him and often did not understand Him. One betrayed Him, another denied Him, and they scattered when He was struck down. He knew all of this would come, but He chose them regardless. Matthew 26:31)

Some version of this is bound to happen in every friendship circle. That friends are inevitable does not mean caution and care in choosing them are unnecessary. As a believer, you will trust, give, forgive, and love the people in your life because that is how God has dealt with you. There is no guarantee that everyone will reciprocate when you conduct yourself with candour and honesty. Often, they will not. Thinking through your selection criteria for whom you keep in your inner circle will reduce the chances that your friends are impediments to your calling and mission.

The first step, incidentally, has nothing to do with other people. It is about taking the time to figure out your calling, vision, and life's mission. These are, in business-speak, three different things, but they are related. To get close to defining these, think about the following:

> ➢ What are you good at?
> ➢ What comes naturally to you that you would be happy to do, even if you did not get paid to do it?

Various sources have discussed the 10 000 hours rule[6], though the number is more of an average than a mark set in stone. It suggests the amount of time that research says it would take to gain expert-level proficiency at something. That is about ten years of work, honing your skills, getting better at pattern recognition, and building your knowledge base around your subject. What area would you be willing to dedicate ten years to the process of just getting better? Indeed, what have you already spent years on? Most of us do what we do because it pays the bills and is the means for us to contribute to the sustenance of our families. If someone fulfilled those responsibilities for you, and you had the opportunity to work on something that is a passion for you, what would that be? What would you want your legacy to be in two or three hundred years?

"What are you genetically encoded for?" is how Jim Collins would phrase it. In discussing the three circles a company can focus on and move from good to great, he directs their thinking toward something they think they can be the best. Being the best can be overwhelming considering the sheer number of people in the same career also aiming for the top spot. There is also the fact that the more specific you get at something, the more you will find success has some particular requirements desire alone will not satisfy. For example, it is almost impossible to make it into the NBA if you are less than 6 feet tall. However, it is possible to be in the top twenty-five percent of whatever you feel you can dedicate yourself to. If you think about it, there are two or three things you can do better than most people. Your job is to find those because when you combine them, you have a combination that will give you a unique perspective if you can figure out how to express it.

Pareto's principle, commonly known as the 80/20 rule[6], is another way you could define your mission and values. If you analyzed your life through this lens, what areas, topics, and activities energize, encourage, inspire, and excite you? The observation that eighty percent of your results come from just twenty percent of what you are doing has been ubiquitous and consistent. The rest falls under things that we must do, or at least what others say is necessary, though they contribute little to the quality of our lives.

These three approaches are merely options for you to choose from. Focused attention on just one of them will be enough. You may have to go through all three to narrow the field. The method is less important than the clarity. Your job is to think through the questions, do some introspection and seek the Lord in prayer. Ask Him to clarify the direction and purpose He created you to fulfil. Once you do, then, like Jesus, that compass helps you decide whom you will keep close.

First Who Then What

Jim Collins' observations go beyond what you are encoded to do and what to do with that information. Once you have an idea of who you are and what your mission might be, he uses a bus analogy to describe the next steps. In a "First Who, Then What" strategy, the leaders that had seen companies through from good to great focused first on getting the wrong people off the bus. Then they got the right people on the bus, taking the time to make sure those people were in the right seats on that bus. Only then was it considered the right time to decide which way the bus would go.

The wrong people in a company do not mesh with the core values and purpose. Some are vocal when they disagree, using their influence to sow dissension. Others keep their thoughts to themselves but never get behind decisions. They are hard to motivate, sap the energy from the team and cost more than they contribute. This is true in your life too. If you analyze your relationships, you will find energizers and depressors. You have those people whose texts and phone calls bring a smile to your face. You also have those whose calls you let go to voicemail, whose texts you plan to respond to later, but somehow you forget to. Then there are those with whom you feel that if you do not reach out to them, there is no relationship at all. These are not evil people, but they are taking up valuable space when it comes to your bus. They are placeholders in a position that people committed to helping and following you on the journey could fill.

You cannot make a good deal with a bad person.[7] So said Warren Buffet in one of his shareholder meetings, providing a window into the practicality of this thought process to business. Some transactions are one-time deals. You might feel the need to let a few deals with bad people happen with no plans or prospects of them happening again. This certainly would have been the case with the king of Sodom and, indeed, Melchizedek. Yet, as the encounters with the two come one after the other in telling Abram's story, there is a crucial lesson to be gleaned from it. When Melchizedek blessed Abram, he used the term "Possessor of heaven and earth" in referring to God. The two never met again. Notice how Abram uses the same name when he is talking to the king of Sodom, "I have raised my hand to the LORD, God Most High, the Possessor of heaven and earth, that I will take nothing, from a thread to a sandal strap, and that I will not take anything that is yours, lest you should say, 'I have made Abram rich.'" (Genesis 14:23)

'You are the aggregate of the five closest people to you.' *Show me your friends, and I'll tell you your character* is another common paraphrase of the bad company corrupts good morals scripture. These feel like a character developing in the general direction influenced by those people *over time.* That Abram goes from one door to the next, as it were, and in between them appropriates "Possessor of heaven and earth" into his own vocabulary says the influence of the people around us is not just time-dependent. Such was the impact of the man Melchizedek and their conversation as they ate together that Abram took something from it and made it his own. One transaction, meeting or visit is enough for one person to influence another. As much as possible, do not make a deal with a person of questionable character. Nothing good can come from it. Instead, surround yourself with good people.

The immediate goal is to have the right people in the right seats. Think of them as your board of directors, a team of coaches, and a set of guides. Based on your criteria, they are people you select to serve you in your quest to fulfil what God has uniquely created you for. Iron sharpens iron. Your sharpness is a non-negotiable part of being effective in your assignment. Getting there requires others whose contributions make you more fitted for your task. There are a few ways to find those people who will sharpen you.

The Red Team

The term red team[8] (or red teaming) builds on the observation that the longer you spend crafting a solution to a problem, the more you fall in love with it. It is as if, as your brainchild, that plan becomes a part of you. It is tied to your self-image. It *is you.* Each of us has the fabled mirror that always answers, 'you are the fairest of them all.' Or perhaps the most qualified or the most skilled. Whatever the quality, it demands validation. As you do that, you ignore the gaps in your plan. You deny its vulnerabilities and go forward as if your proposal came from God Himself. Enter the red team—a group of people to whom you tell your brilliant plan and then permit them to tear it to shreds. If you asked them, "How would you disrupt this plan" and let them put it through a rigorous stress test, you would avoid the trap of falling in love with your ideas while ignoring their weaknesses. How do they become red team members?

Humility

Look for people who are humble and coachable. The effect the wrong people have on you is always a question of their ability to listen, open their minds and see that there is a better way to do things. Observe the people you may be thinking about for the seats on your bus. How do they take criticism? Observe the questions they ask when things are going well and when they are not. Would you want to be coached by someone who isn't coachable? Would you like to have someone who handles criticism poorly offer you criticism?

Experience

Never take advice from someone you would not trade places with. This idea is about getting experience on your team. Melchizedek, little as we know about him, was a priest of God Most High. He had a relationship with God, and though we all remain children before Him, one might say Melchizedek was older, if not a little farther along on his journey than Abram. The lesser, according to the book of Hebrews, was blessed by the better. You will benefit from having someone senior to you too. Who has been where you want to go? What can you learn from them? This mentor would be one-third of the recommendation from Chris Fussell[9], a former Navy Seal and senior executive at a leadership consulting firm. In his words, "I always work to have a senior mentor in my life that I look up to, a peer whom I think is doing things better than me, and someone younger who I think is living life more effectively than I was at that age. Keep a running list of people in these categories that you can watch and learn from."

Integrity

Integrity is soundness and resolution in your values in the face of perturbations. It is the ability to, having defined your principles, stand by them regardless of the forces pulling or pushing you from that position. In many research studies, integrity is used synonymously with character. In that view, it is about being a person who is truthful, ethical, and principled. Everyone can feign uprightness, but you need people of the highest integrity on your board. To come to your decisions, these are the people you will be bouncing some of your ideas on, depending on their experience, networks, and opinions. To figure out the measure of someone's integrity, check out his reputation. Job hopefuls (used to) include references on a résumé. The potential employer would call them to verify one or two facts. You may have to do something similar. What do friends and colleagues say about this person? Is he the stand-by-you type of person? Is she the same person in public as in private, or does she put on an act? General Stanley McCrystal[10] has a couple of bold questions that get to the heart of the matter, directed at the person you are considering.

Say you are thinking of having Joshua on your board. You might say, "Everyone says Josh is great, but..." the ensuing silence is what you want to see. In that time, Josh's wheels will be turning. You have forced him into articulating how he feels others perceive him. He must come to terms with what people do not love about him and find the courage to say it to your face. Related but more direct is the question, "What will people who don't hold you in the highest regard say about you?" Having an answer to this tells you about Josh's level of self-awareness. There can be no growth in any area of life without self-awareness. This is the first step of emotional intelligence, a subject we will discuss in the second section of this book. If someone does not have an answer to these questions, he may not deserve a seat on your bus. The right person will say whatever his critics may have to say and, without trying to say it is not valid, will at least suggest by being aware of it and working on it.

Advisors and Interests

The Bible indicates what happens when your closest advisers are short on integrity. King Darius was forced to use his seal to condemn his friend Daniel to the lion's den because he was not diligent in evaluating the character of his advisers. Daniel distinguished himself above the governors and satraps because an excellent spirit was in him, and the king wanted to reward him. He gave thought to set him over the whole realm and voiced his idea, but it only stirred jealousy. So the governors and satraps looked to find some charge against Daniel concerning the kingdom, but they could not because he was faithful.

Other versions say they could find no corruption in him because he was trustworthy and neither corrupt nor negligent. Daniel was a man of integrity. He was as upright as they were crooked. They had to invent a law because nothing else could help them achieve their sinister goal. Then they stroked the king's ego into enforcing that law. It was not until the consequences of that decision played themselves out that King Darius saw what he had done. Some of the ideas in this book are hoping that implementing them will save you his trouble. He was distressed and was forced into a frenzy, trying to undo what he had done before the sun went down. The only good thing that one could say for him was that his period of torture was a short one. He went without food and entertainment that night, which was very unusual for a king. More familiar to the rest of us, he could not sleep with anxiety, regret, and remorse. (Daniel 6:1-23)

In contrast, Aaron and Hur climbed the mountain with Moses as Joshua led the armies of Israel against the army of Amalek.

They could not wield his staff for him, but their interests aligned with his, and they did what they could. While Moses' hands were up, the Israelites prevailed. They lost ground when his hands got tired. So Aaron and Hur allowed themselves to be pillars. Moses could rest his arms on them. When his legs were tired, they found a stone for him to sit on. They did everything they could to make Moses comfortable. Their success was his, and that benefited the soldiers on the ground. (Exodus 17:8-13)

It was a sense of purpose, of understanding what was important that helped Abram and Melchizedek see in one another a fellow worshipper. These explain why they shared a meal, why Melchizedek blessed Abram and why Abram gave him tithes. This is made much clearer by Abram's refusal to accept a gift from the king of Sodom. Abram was careful about whom he was associating with because he knew those people would be in his story. Their reputations would sully his. This is true for you too.

9

THE DISCIPLINE OF NO

Abram's path was not smooth, and yours will not be either. Family drama, famines and temptations were part of his story, and they will take their shape in yours. He held the promises God had made (he would inherit the land and his seed will be blessed) close to him, making things easier than they could have been. This book contends that as you walk with God, your calling is your compass on your journey. Defining that as precisely as you can is the true north, and if you keep that before you, you will eventually get to the promised land.

How you will reach the place God has called you to is a highly personal matter that is not likely to be discovered in a book. What can be taken from these pages is the advice from others who have completed theirs. The author of Hebrews references the lives of many saints and bids us to imitate their faith. (Hebrews 6:12) Among the things they did to help them was the discipline of saying no.

The matter of kings fighting each other had nothing to do with Abram. He had gone out not to meddle in those affairs. He had no allegiance to any of them, so his presence was a declaration of siding with one side or the other. Abram's mission was to rescue his nephew. It just happened that he had to fight off Sodom's enemies to do so. Abram would have been within reason to accept, even demand a gift. When offered one, he refused it. Abram, it seems, had not only adopted Melchizedek's name for God, but he had also taken his blessing. "Blessed be Abram of God Most High." (Genesis 14:19) Abram refused the gift not only because he did not need it, but he had also decided God was the source of his riches. "Lest you should say, 'I have made Abram rich" was not about the king of Sodom as much as it was about that compass. (Genesis 14:23)

Hedgehogs and Boundaries

To get the place God has called you, to achieve what He has assigned, you will need to develop the ability to say no to good opportunities. In the "Good to Great" story, Jim Collins found what he and his coauthors called the hedgehog concept.1

Suppose you were able to construct a work-life that meets the following three tests. Imagine each of the points is in a circle. First, you are doing work for which you have a genetic or God-given talent, and you could become one of the best in the world (top 25%) in applying that talent. As we looked at before, the higher the pinnacle, the easier it will be for you to feel overwhelmed and disqualify yourself. If you are having trouble deciding what that is, ask yourself, when do you think "I was just born to be doing this." Are there any activities or tasks that others might have said you were born to do?

Second, you are paid well for what you do. This one feels like a dream that somehow you have won the lottery. The third point is like it: you are doing work you are for which you are passionate. Your love for it simply oozes out of you when you talk about your work. It's a subject you could go on about all day. It is the kind of work rewarding in the process and the results when you think about it.

If you were to overlap the three circles, your personal Hedgehog Concept is where they meet. If you could translate whatever is in that intersection into a simple, crystalline concept, you could use that to guide your choices. It is here where the discipline of saying no comes in.

To continue to be among the crème in your area, you will need to hold tightly to your concept and reject anything beyond it. Like Joseph, no matter how attractive the prospect of being with Potiphar's wife may be, you need to say no regardless of how appealing the opportunity may appear. Indeed, you must flee from it. He had no way of knowing he would end up in the palace, second only to Pharoah. Yet, giving in to that temptation was, for him, a sin against God (Genesis 39:9) and a departure from the path of integrity. There are occasions when it would not be a sin to indulge. There could be "nothing wrong" with grabbing hold of any opportunity. It may even be good to linger and get involved just a little.

Having spent the night healing many who were sick with various diseases and casting out many demons, Jesus went out and left to a solitary place to pray early the following morning. When Simon and the other disciples noticed He was gone, they searched for Him. When they found Him, they said to Him, "Everyone is looking for You." (Mark 1: 35-39) They had seen firsthand everything He was doing. They could see the joy and the relief of those He had ministered to. They had heard Him preach and could feel the impact it was having.

Most importantly, they were seeing evidence of John's claim that Jesus was the Messiah. As the disciples believed, they wanted others to share their belief, and they were excited as crowds began to gather in the morning. It must have come as a surprise to them when He responded, "Let us go into the next towns, that I may preach there also." He was doing good, and the people were clamouring for more. Yet, He wanted to go elsewhere. By His decision, many would be disappointed. Some would not be healed that day unless they followed Him to the towns He was going to. His purpose, He said, was to preach the good news in the other cities and cities, not just that one place. To accomplish what He came to do, Jesus said no to staying longer where He was, where people had already accepted Him.

Pick Carefully

The story of Apple is incomplete without the awkward bit in which Steve Jobs,2 having co-founded the company, was fired from it, only to be asked back years later. In his first year back, the fiscal year that ended when Jobs became interim CEO in September 1997, Apple lost $1.04 billion (about $3 per person in the US). In his mind, it was because of a lack of focus on the company's thinking and its products.

When Steve took the helm, Apple had a dozen versions of the Macintosh, with a very confusing cataloguing system. After three weeks, he had people explain it to him, and he still could not figure it out. He tried simplifying things. "Which ones do I tell my friends to buy?" When even that approach could not get him closer to understanding it, Jobs began slashing away at models and products. Soon he had cut 70% of them. He grabbed a magic marker at one big product strategy session, padded to a whiteboard, and drew a four-squared chart. "Here's what we need," he continued. Atop the two columns, he wrote "Consumer" and "Pro"; he labelled the two rows "Desktop" and "Portable." Their job, he said, was to make four great products, one for each quadrant.

The sharper focus imposed by Jobs' quadrant meant the company would have to get out of other businesses. In 1997, Apple was in the business of servers and printers, which they sold together with HP ink cartridges. In the middle of another product review meeting, having decided it did not make sense for them to continue down that road, Jobs left the room and called the head of HP. When he got back, he announced Apple was pulling out of the printer business entirely, leaving HP to produce the machines and the ink. Jobs met with the dozens of product teams at Apple and, in the same way, asked them to justify going ahead with their products.

This ability to focus saved Apple. For the full fiscal year of 1998, just one year after Jobs' return, the company turned in a $309 million profit. People think focus means saying yes to what you must focus on, but, according to Steve Jobs, that is not what it means. It means saying no to a hundred other promising ideas that exist. You must pick carefully.

The benefit of focusing, especially when presented in monetary form, is plain. The "secret" of those who accomplish much is deciding what must get their attention and what does not. They say no to many opportunities that others say yes to. They only take in what falls inside their hedgehog concept and resist the distractions of whatever is newest, shiniest, or most popular. They do only one thing at a time. As a result, they need much less time to achieve their goals in the end than the rest of us. In short, the more one can concentrate time, effort, and resources, the greater the number and diversity of tasks one can perform.

⌶ Pressured into Yes

The opposite is, of course, saying yes to every opportunity. It is one of the standard practices of today. Despite many hacks, gadgets and technological advancements, productivity is not higher. Everyone is busy, but few are getting things done, and of those, only a fraction is producing anything of quality. If you want to be effective, make good decisions, and craft your life, you must be more deliberate. Decide which tasks, people and opportunities deserve priority and which are less critical. The only question is which will decide—you or the various pressures in your life? One of the most crippling pressures is the fear of missing out. Some people say yes to everything and everyone because they are afraid the commitment to one thing means they will miss the other things they are no longer available to do. Unfortunately, their approach to mitigating that potential loss is to say yes to every opportunity but, in so doing, overextend themselves. As they give time and energy and pour emotionally into all those commitments, the simultaneous slowly depletes them. They are involved in many things, but none of them gets their full attention.

To assume every opportunity could make you equally happy is ludicrous. It is similarly foolish to think every challenge will be equally stressful. It is this inability to differentiate between options that make this so costly. "A man cannot serve two masters," said Jesus. (Matthew 6:24) He meant any attempt to do so denies both masters love and loyalty, the two things that turn into a reward for the servant. If you chase two rabbits, you will catch neither.

Time is another source of pressure that often makes the decisions for those who have not developed the discipline to stay within their hedgehog concept. Failure to define values, one's mission and focusing on that can be like a snowball rolling downhill. You are left with no boundaries to narrow your options, but you also have no sense of priorities because everything is equally important. You decide not according to the priorities of your calling but to alleviate the sense of urgency. You do what is urgent rather than what is essential. You will join the throng of those who fill their days doing what is critical for other people while making no progress on their own calling, mission, and purpose.

How is your task list populated? How do you decide which order to tackle that list? What determines how you address the requests in your inbox?

You cannot reach God's highest and best for you if you do not know how to set priorities. This idea has been around for centuries, yet most are still unable to reap its benefits. It may be because most reduced the concept to simply numbering items on a list. The numbers in themselves, however, are impotent. By sheer force of nature, something must come first on the page if you write things down. Often, it is merely subject to availability bias—what comes first and easily to mind. When this is stirred in the decision-making process with time pressure, what most people consider their priorities are simply those things that are urgent among the things they can remember. The effort to design your decisions is an attempt to systematically focus on the things that fall within your three circles.

The urgency of hunger saw Esau trade his birthright for a bowl of soup. (Genesis 25:29-34) In contrast, a sense of what was important inspired the conquered Hebrew boys to respond, "O Nebuchadnezzar, we have no need to answer you in this matter. If that is the case, our God whom we serve is able to deliver us from the burning fiery furnace, and He will deliver us from your hand, O king. But if not, let it be known to you, O king, that we do not serve your gods, nor will we worship the gold image which you have set up." (Daniel 3:16-18) Their urgent need was for deliverance from the threat to their lives, but they decided to address what was eternal instead of temporal.

Sticking to the decision

This chapter has been about knowing when to say no, just as Abram did with the king of Sodom. The job, however, is not to set priorities. It is much easier to draw up a nice list of items, number them and call them your "top priorities." Hedging—trying to do "just a little bit" of everything on the list—could make you feel good. The only drawback is that nothing of quality gets done. The issue then is not in how to analyse the list but in deciding what tasks not to tackle and sticking to the decision—courage rather than fancy analysis is the order of the day.

Peter Drucker offered the following rules for identifying priorities:[3]

Pick the future against the past.

There is much to learn from what has already happened in your life and others'. It is prudent to study history and learn from it. The key, however, is to retain its lessons but leave the past in the past. "Do not remember the former things, nor consider the things of old. Behold, I will do a new thing. Now it shall spring forth- shall you not know it?" (Isaiah 43:18-19)

Focus on opportunity rather than on the problem.

You will have to work hard to overcome the natural tendency to zero in on the things that are not working well. This point can easily be construed as "ignore or don't address your problems", but that is not what it means at all. Instead, it means to look for the opportunity *in the issue*. With that lens, the situation becomes the fertile ground for the next breakthrough, idea and innovation. Lazarus' death was the opportunity Jesus needed to teach that He was the Resurrection and the life. He needed to prepare His disciples for the day when He would rise from the dead. The two-day delay after getting the message that Lazarus was sick was intentional. Nothing was as potent as a body that had started to decay- proof to everyone that Lazarus was dead, rather than being in some transitory state that might be used as a counterargument. The completeness of this miracle allowed Jesus to point His disciples forward and lay the foundation for the hope that we have that death is not the end.

Similarly, the people's hunger in the desert was a real problem.

That much is evident, judging by how the disciples approached Jesus. The gospels tell us that Jesus was not alarmed, even after they told Him all they had in supply was a boy's packed lunch. He fed the five thousand men, besides women and children, with the five loaves and two fish. When we meditate on the Lord's provision, we think of this miracle. By doing so, Jesus augmented the proofs illustrated in the oil and the flour that did not run out in the days of Elisha and Elijah. He is our Provider, and He took this scarcity opportunity to illustrate that.

Looking at the opportunity rather than the problem is not just about miracles. The right people on the right seats strategy is about integrity, fit within the company culture, alignment with your vision, team players, and other character-based requirements. Skills or degrees are the last things people look for when hiring. Otherwise, there would never be multiple candidates vying for the same job. A child with boundless energy who seems more disruptive in class may indicate that homeschooling may be a better route for their education. Promotions also depend on emotional intelligence abilities, which appear throughout this book, including the ability to manage people. Focusing on the opportunities might look like recognising someone's skills and moving them to a different seat on the bus. That comes from asking how someone works best, what their strengths are and whether the challenges they are having are because those things don't align with the tasks of their current position.

Finally, consider the following problem. A business looking at its books to evaluate its efforts to get a foothold in a new region finds an area struggling. The salespeople in that city section are not selling as many products as expected. Another section reports that a different part of the city also shows results contrary to expectations. The team from that area reports new opportunities uncaptured in the original projections. Imagine you are the leader in charge of this business. Where will you send your best people to the struggling area or the untapped potential? Do you expend resources to get a sub-standard section to a pass mark, or do you send them where you can convert your business from good to great?

Choose your direction—rather than climb on the bandwagon.

Anything and everything extraordinary begins with the decision to break from the norm. To be a follower of Jesus is to swim the current. Obeying His commands and following Jesus' example is nothing but the opposite of the bandwagon. He models meekness, prays for His enemies, and makes Himself a servant to all. He washes the feet of the disciple He knows will betray Him.

The specific direction depends on what God has called you to achieve and where He has commissioned you to go. As such, it is not something someone else can tell you. You must discover it as you walk with Him. Expect the things you hear to be contrarian. The decision that changes everything is the commitment to that contrarian way of life as He commands it.

Remember where we started: Abraham was on his own path the moment he decided there was more to life than the idols of his forebears. He was the first Jew; the individual God chose to begin the lineage of Christ.

Aim high. Aim for something that will make a difference, rather than what is "safe" and easy to do.

It is never clear what will happen in the future. Uncertainty is unsettling, and it makes people want to do something, anything, just to feel like they have some control over their lives. That need for control is among the most potent factors that eliminate their ability to discriminate between opportunities. It does not make much sense to say no to something right before you when there is no guarantee that something else will come along. Of course, that is an earthly perspective.

God's plans for you, the thoughts of peace, to give you a future and hope, do not just happen. You need to go on offence, beginning with saying no, even to good opportunities. Create the time to focus, learn the things you want to know, build what you want to develop, and invest in relationships you want to grow. God's best for you will require all of that, but it results from a singular focus on what He has called you to do.

10

YOUR EXCEEDINGLY
GREAT REWARD

While Abram felt he would "take nothing, from a thread to a sandal strap" (Genesis 14:23), he did not shut the door for others. He told the king of Sodom to let the others have their share. This is leadership in action. According to Simon Sinek, Leaders eat last.[1] Abram acknowledged the risk his men took in following him. He did not want or need the gift, but there was no reason for them not to enjoy the spoils. Saying yes to Melchizedek and no to the king of Sodom did not just keep Abram within his hedgehog concept. It was not just about associating with the right people. God's response in the next chapter illustrates the full impact of Abram's choice to forego his rightful spoils of war.

The Bible does not say how much time passed between the two incidences. The chapter and verse divisions are recent, making finding what we are looking for easier. The separation between chapters fourteen and fifteen makes their contents seem like separate stories. Chapter 15 stresses it was "after these things." It makes sense as it references Abram's encounters with Melchizedek and the king of Sodom. Understand that you may not see the rewards of your choices immediately, whether in that moment or years after. Like a seed sown, the fruit of every decision will bear fruit.

⬆ Invitations

"After these things, the word of the LORD came to Abram in a vision, saying, "Do not be afraid, Abram. I am your shield, your exceedingly great reward" (Genesis 15:1).

God's response to Abram's choice is stunning. Because Abram would not take the reward offered by men, preferring that no one get the credit for making him rich, God gave him something even more valuable. The Lord announces Himself as Abram's shield in direct response to the fact that Abram had just returned from war. A battle like the one he had to engage in to rescue his nephew Lot would never happen over him. God would stand between Abram and any enemy that would revolt against him. God also promised him a great reward sparking a question, a promise, that sows the seed for the birth of a nation and something entirely unheard of in all of history.

Chapter 15 is a transition chapter. In this story of Abram, years since the Lord called to him, this is the first record of a conversation between him and God. Up to this point, the LORD speaks to Abram, and he obeys (Chapter 12), or he builds an altar and calls on His name. But now there is a back-and-forth, an exchange. Their relationship is changed: it is more profound, more intimate, and more personal. It has changed, so the Lord and servant dynamic coexists with a friend-to-friend side as well. Abram learns that God's real end game is closeness, which Jesus would later pray for, "That they all may be one, as You, Father, are in Me, and I in You; that they also may be one in Us... And the glory which You gave Me I have given them, that they may be one just as We are one: I in them, and You in Me; that they may be made perfect in one, and that the world may know that You have sent Me, and have loved them as You have loved Me." (John 17:21-23)

Abram had to find the courage to be vulnerable to align himself with God and begin to draw close to Him. The gods he had left behind were not gods at all. They were images that could neither hear nor speak, much less be concerned enough to act in the lives of those who worshipped them. But this God, the "Possessor of heaven and earth", was different. Would Abram act differently, too? Would he have the courage to cry out from his heart? Would he be brave enough to lay out his deepest desire expectantly and boldly to the God he believed in?

"But Abram said, 'Lord GOD, what will You give me, seeing I go childless, and the heir of my house is Eliezer of Damascus?' Then Abram said, 'Look, You have given me no offspring; indeed, one born in my house is my heir!'" (Genesis 15:2-3)

Abram took God's offer of Himself as his "exceedingly great reward" as an invitation to a deeper level of relationship. It emboldened him to zoom in on what he wanted and tell God about it. He wanted an heir, a child of his own. This was his lifelong dream—but Sarai was barren. Abram had arrived at a fork in the road. He could continue to skirt around the issue, remaining disappointed but safe. Or he could take a chance. Sarai was the love of his life, but she could not bear a child. Would he challenge reality with the God of creation wooing him into a relationship? Would he shed the shackles of fact and ask God regardless?

This is a crucial consideration in decision-making. There is always a moment just before you commit one way or another in which mindfulness can be of immense benefit. As you weigh your options, ask yourself, am I choosing to stay where I am comfortable or am I willing to risk everything that comes with being courageous? For a long time, the message that courage is the absence of fear rang from every platform. That view gives fear an inordinate amount of power because the natural response to it is fight or flight, and between them, the former is more common. Abram's urge is to lean into what is scary, uncomfortable, and full of the potential for failure and even rejection. He, like you, had no guarantee that he would do what he wanted. The courage is in the asking. God said, "You do not have because you do not ask." (James 4:3) You can shrink away from asking because there is a chance you will not receive what you want—flight. Or you can ask, aware of the possibility of getting a "no" but also knowledge of the guarantee you will not receive if you do not ask—fight. Every decision has some promise and possibility or a greater chance of one and lesser of another.

After publishing the prospect theory, Daniel Kahneman[2] won the Nobel Prize in economics. After doing a series of experiments and considering the psychological and emotional patterns behind what he saw, he proposed that the brain seems to feel a loss at least twice emotionally and psychologically impactful as an equivalent gain. Through scenarios and conundrums set up by hypothetical questions, he discovered people were more motivated to avoid losing money than they were to make the same amount. They "worked" harder to avoid losing $20 than to make $20. They took at least twice the number of risks to protect what they had than make the same amount.

The Fourfold Pattern

Kahneman broke the observed behaviours into categories known as the fourfold pattern. Most often represented as quadrants, prospect theory suggests the following:

Q1: In general, people will tend to pick the safer choice when there is a high chance they will get what they want. This is the "It's better to have something than nothing" line of thinking. It is also what makes us think it is better not to take a chance at a relationship because that way, you cannot get hurt. Love is a gamble, and so is faith. Our tendency to want a sure thing is human, but it costs us in these high-probability, high-gain situations because we want to avoid risk. As a result, we miss some of the things we crave.

In Q2 is the "double or nothing" line of thinking. It is the arena where the most obvious thing about the situation is desperate, but rather than give it up, they throw everything at it, even when they know the hope of getting what they want is slim. There are situations such as it was with the woman with the issue of blood. Going to find Jesus was her last chance effort. It worked out. Others will similarly pour their life savings into financing an experimental treatment plan in the hope of a few more years with a terminally ill loved one. It does not always turn out as it did in the Bible, but you feel for them and understand how someone could do that in these situations. In similar cases, businesses have gone bankrupt, struggling with the sunk cost fallacy. This is when you consider how much time, effort, money, and sacrifices have gone into the project or business. When it is all too much, it seems reasonable to do everything you can to rescue the situation, to make it all mean something. You never want to look back and say it was "all for nothing", so you pour more into it. Just one last effort. The final push- a more extensive investment. Sadly, this approach typically leads to disastrous consequences. Q2 is a high-probability, big-losses category.

In Q3, we discovered that dreaming has a higher price than you might expect. Here, there is the promise of something big, a chance to win the lottery, a car, a house or maybe a holiday. The costs come in when you consider how much you would be willing to pay for a chance to win the pipe dream. A lottery ticket is just a Christmas stocking stuffer for some because it's a tradition. For others, it is a small investment, a dollar or two every time they go grocery shopping. That adds up through the months and years. People are willing to pay a premium for the opportunity to wish and dream despite the low, minuscule probability that they will win. With a low barrier to entry, scores of people across the country are also buying multiple tickets hoping to increase their chances of winning. The disappointment when it turns out you are just 2 or 3 digits somehow is not a deterrent. Despite knowing that buying another ticket will not get you closer to winning, you cannot help yourself—just one more, then another, and another. Unconsciously and cumulatively, most people spend more than they will ever win.

Q4: Amazingly, where we usually shy away from the courageous, risky choice, we have a proclivity to pay premium prices to ensure we do not lose, even when the chances of that loss are low. With responsible and proper adjustments such as paying attention to the following distance and changing tires and chains (low probability- significant loss), winter driving is not significantly more dangerous than summer. Sliding is undoubtedly a factor, but the number of injuries and fatalities is not alarmingly different from other seasons of the year. While the statistics show a low rate of injury and deaths, the availability bias comes into play. Weather reports, buoyed by live video, show cars in ditches (and some parked off the road by their owners!) and stress the difficult driving conditions. News bulletins notice any accidents and cycle them repeatedly for days. What is driving like in the winter? Dangerous. However, many people are willing to forego meeting their families for Christmas or any other event that involves travelling on perceived treacherous roads. People are willing to pay a premium for the certainty of not losing. It's the same reason we pay the unreasonable prices we do for insurance. We are buying peace of mind, paying to think and feel we have done what we could to minimize the things we are anxious about and the impact they may have on our lives.

One of the reasons we have so many biases and the brain takes the shortcuts it does is that we are unaware of them. Our tendencies for risk-taking at certain times (Q2, Q3) and being risk-averse at others (Q1, Q4) are just observations. Rather than telling you this is what you are *going to do* because you do not have a choice, they are decision points on which you can capitalize.

The following are not prescriptive but suggestions: when you are in the spotlight, slow down and allow yourself the chance to decide rather than react to situations.

> ➤ Is this a high-probability, big-gain situation? Be strong and courageous and lean in, rather than letting the desire for comfort force you to settle for less.
> ➤ Is this a low-probability, big-gain situation? Recognize it is a lottery and shift your investments inside your hedgehog concept.
> ➤ Is this a high-probability, big-loss situation? You want to know whether doubling down will make things worse and sink the ship. Or is it better to cut your losses? Beware the sunken cost fallacy.
> ➤ Is this a low-probability, big-loss situation? The cost of life insurance and a will are worth the peace of mind they give you. Are there areas where you could be courageous? Are there relationships that you could reconcile? What opportunities are you missing, paralyzed by a "what if" that has a low probability of happening?

Abram took the courageous way. He leaned into the vulnerable moment, and God rewarded him for it.

But Abram said, "Lord GOD, what will You give me, seeing I go childless, and the heir of my house is Eliezer of Damascus?" Then Abram said, "Look, You have given me no offspring; indeed, one born in my house is my heir!"

And behold, the word of the LORD came to him, saying, "This one shall not be your heir, but one who will come from your own body shall be your heir." (Genesis 15:2-4)

11

HE BELIEVED

"And he believed in the LORD, and He accounted it to him for righteousness" (Genesis 15:6)

This text is key to all things Christian. The rest of the Bible is the who, what, and how of righteousness, but it all begins (and ends) here—God speaks, you believe. Anything else complicates what God designed to be simple; it makes impossible what God made possible and burdensome what He means to be easy and light.

The critical text comes after Abram has asked God for his *one thing*: an heir. God tells him He would answer that request with not just one from his own body but as many as the stars. Abram believed the Lord. The father of many nations is also the father of faith.

Traditionally, we offer a section of Paul's letter to the Romans as the solution to any unbelief or doubt. "How then can they call on the One in whom they have not believed? And how can they believe in the One of whom they have not heard? And how can they hear without someone to preach? And how can they preach unless they are sent? As it is written: "How beautiful are the feet of those who bring good news!" (Romans 10:14-15) We assume that faith will grow if we just read the Bible more, quote Scripture, walk around saying things to ourselves (affirmations), or remind each other about relevant stories.

Anybody who has walked with the LORD for any length of time knows there is more to believing than hearing things repeatedly. As much as we would like it to, "Do not be afraid," does not make us less fearful, anxious, or braver. Pointing out how frequently the Bible repeats specific commands or words is excellent for emphasis. But knowing how often "by faith" is found throughout the Bible does not engender more faith. So how do you come to the point of believing? What happened to/in Abraham that God counted his response as righteousness? He believed.

Believing is a multi-step process, which suggests multiple stages where we can get stuck. Consider the following framework:
Believing = Credibility + Communication + Commitment

Credibility

Believing requires the subject to have credibility or that the message has some. This view alone confirms what you might find if you look in the dictionary for a definition of the word "believe." The credibility of the witnesses decides court cases. The more we feel we can trust somebody and that their view is reliable, the more confident we have that their testimony is honest and true. Therefore, many of the commands in Scripture are prefixed or suffixed with, "I am the LORD (your God)." He set up His authority and the grounds on which to say such a thing. (Ex: 20:2; Num 3:13; Lev 26:45; Is 44:6.) The prophets used the same formula, "Thus says the LORD." Today, we simply say, "Jesus said," or, "the Bible says," and our audience at once holds what follows in higher esteem than what comes across as mere opinion. If you do not believe the messenger, you will not believe the message. In one form or another, this feeling is pervasive and consistent whether people verbally express that sentiment or not. It is so vital it is the first law of leadership from decades of research by Kouzes and Posner.[3]

Communication

Credible witnesses who are inappropriately emotional, contradictory, or offensive in how they communicate will lose credibility, believability and influence. Emotions seep into our communication whether we are on the speaking end or listening end. When your communication proves you are paying attention, that you are interested in what others have to say, how they feel, and how they see the world, you show yourself as trustworthy. At that point, they are more likely to be willing to hear you out. This is what Jesus meant when He said, "And just as you want men to do to you, you also do to them likewise." (Luke 6:31) We have traditionally considered this to mean seeing how you would react/see things/or what you would ask for in the same situation as someone else. There is much more to it than that, and Jesus showed that extra level Himself.

"Father, forgive them, for they do not know what they do," Jesus asked as He prayed for those who had tried and convicted Him. (Luke 23: 32-35) They had flogged and crucified Him, and, as He hung between two criminals, they were casting lots for His clothes at His feet. They mocked Him, saying, "He saved others; let Him save Himself", and gave Him vinegar when He was thirsty. Why would anyone seek forgiveness for people treating Him like that? Jesus considered the world from their perspective.

Think about the energy, time, and money you spent to earn your degree. Think about the sacrifices you made to get there. Remember how hard you had to work and graduate, only to start working somewhere and be at the bottom of the ladder. The road ahead would be one in which you would have to prove yourself repeatedly. Imagine having finally made it to the top, having carved yourself a reputation among your colleagues and in your community, and you can have a say in how the running of things. At that moment, some young, new guy comes along, threatening all of that. Not only is your respect among the people at stake, but also everything you have worked hard to build—the compromises, the constantly having to make the best of terrible situations—all of it could go out the window if this new movement takes root.

How would you feel? What ideas would you have in deciding how to deal with the situation? As a religious leader, how would you respond to someone subverting the people, threatening the fragile peace with the Romans? Would you sit by and watch while a young rabbi from one of the worst cities in Israel, who had not gone to any recognized school, teaches the people the oral traditions and interpretations of the law that have been the mainstay of the people for generations are wrong?

When you read the Bible, you benefit from hindsight and foresight. You do not know the story of Jesus any other way than that He died and rose again. You read the book of Mark beginning with, "This is the beginning of the gospel of Jesus Christ, the Son of God." (Mark 1:1) You read this already, knowing and believing that He is the Son of God. The people among whom Jesus walked did not. They did not realize that they had the right to eternal life by believing in His sacrificial death. Jesus knew this about His contemporaries, and though He expressed His frustration that they were slow to understand and accept, He did not hold it against them. If they could see into eternity and understand the Father's plan, the Son's role in it and how their choices affected their future, He might have held them to a different standard. But in coming to dwell among us, Jesus knew their worldview. He tried to influence it, and after He returned to heaven, His Spirit would continue the work of transforming their minds. Until the Lord has exhausted effort is made in this direction, He will not hold our actions against us any more than you would against a child who got into stuff he should not have but did not know any better. As He prayed the Father would forgive them, the most significant piece of evidence, His resurrection, had not been given yet. Would He treat them as if it had?

This is what the Golden Rule is. It is laying aside your perspective and adopting the other. It is to see, feel and experience the other person's view to the best of your ability and ask from that place, what would I like from others if this was how I saw things if this was what these things meant to me? By His prayer, Jesus showed He understood them, me, and you. "For in that He Himself has suffered, being tempted, He is able to aid those who are tempted." (Hebrews 2:18)

The Bible is a collection of stories that chronicles God's involvement in our world and lives. It communicates His love and care. Only when we accept these words and stories as accurate and let the weight of that impact our lives will the Scriptures affect us as God intended.

Commitment

Commitment is both abandonment and attachment. When you find someone who is credible and accept that what they are communicating is in your best interest, you feel better about moving forward with them. And to do that, you must leave behind the anchorage you already have to take a step forward. No story illustrates this quite the same way as Peter's walking on water.8

Imagine being there yourself, watching as a ghost walks on water toward you. Except, of course, you do not believe in ghosts. So seeing the ghost tells you how hard your brain is working to make sense of what your eyes are telling you. But in typical fashion, Jesus says, "Don't be afraid. It is I."

"Lord, if it is You," Peter replied, "command me to come to you on the water."

He was leaning on the first part of the process: credibility. He was convinced Jesus was the Son of God. He had seen miracles happen simply by the power of His word. If He gave the word, the impossible would be possible, and he, Peter, would be able to walk on water too.

"Come."

And suddenly, a man who had been on the seas his whole life was doing something he would never have dreamed. At least, that is what it would seem like if you just read the text as it is.

'Then Peter got down out of the boat, walked on the water, and came toward Jesus." (Matthew 14:22-33)

But something happened between the command, "Come!" and the act of getting down off the boat. Peter had asked for that very thing as proof that it was Jesus, not some ghost. Now that Jesus had given the invitation, would Peter back out? Would he say, never mind? No. He had to commit. He had to trust what he expected would happen, that Jesus would not have called him out if walking on water was something only He could do. He had to let that conviction energize his senses and move. Peter had to get out of the boat. Only then would he be able to prove the efficacy of Jesus' word and, by extension, get the evidence that it was Jesus.

You cannot walk on water and be in the boat simultaneously. Faith without action is dead. Action proves faith. (James 2:14-26) Paul adds a further dimension, "Whatsoever is not of faith is sin." (Romans 14:23) In a way, believing gives you "no choice." Peter had to step out of the boat, and it had to be on faith. And once on the water, he had no choice but to go toward Jesus; taking a couple of steps then returning to the boat was not an option.

That Peter began to sink was not because he suddenly noticed the strength of the wind. In setting the scene, the Bible tells us the waves buffeted the boat because the wind was against it. For a career fisherman, Peter would have been very aware of the wind patterns and the effect they have on the water. It is one thing to understand and "ride out" the waves when in a boat. It is entirely different to figure out how to navigate yourself when you are *in* the water. Swimming is a skill every fisher needs to be proficient at to make a career out of it. Peter, however, was *on* the water, walking on it. This unknown is what made Peter lose focus. He still believed Jesus was the Son of God and that His word had the power to make him walk on water. But in considering the strength of the wind, Peter lost the confidence that he could do it, even if all the other conditions were ripe for it to happen. He doubted just a little. He stood on the water but not in faith.

Posture

When can you say you believe? Only when you decide to leave behind some perspective because of God's credibility, whatever the words He has spoken are for your good and do as He says. When you trust Him enough to let go of your worldview and adopt His view of you, your past, present and future, you will take on a new posture that reflects that. Only after that commitment can you say you believe.

So what happened to Abram? What would you expect to see when you tell your hungry child you are preparing food for her? You see them adopt a different posture. She does not have the agitation or tenseness of not knowing how and when her hunger will be satisfied. She is calm and expectant. Her behaviour shows it. The same thing happened with Abram. He believed the God who called Him from his father's house and kept him thus far could be a shield for him. Abram perceived in what God was saying a desire to bless him. His demeanour showed it. He believed God, and He counted it to him for righteousness. (Genesis 15:6)

12

---◆──○──➤---

SIMPLIFY

And behold, the word of the LORD came to him, saying, "...
one who will come from your own body shall be your heir...
[Like the stars] So shall your descendants be." And he believed in
the LORD, and He accounted it to him for righteousness. Then
He said to him, "I am the LORD, who brought you out of Ur of the
Chaldeans, to give you this land to inherit it." And he said, "Lord
GOD, how shall I know that I will inherit it?" (Genesis 15:4-8)

It is normal to be robust, steadfast, solid, and have faith
unquestionable in one area but needs some proof in other areas.
Even the father of faith had to ask God, "How will I know?"

The strange thing is comparing where he believes almost
automatically and where he needs proof. On the other side of 80
years old, somehow, God's promise that his heir would be a child
from his own body was believable, but inheriting the land, he was
living in was a little more complicated. Why is that?

It was not unusual for men to have children late in their years,
though the trend was changing. Abram stands for the twentieth
generation from Adam. Of all those men before him, eight had
had their first-born sons older than Abram was at this point in his

life. The genealogies in the Bible also suggest that other children were born at ages far more advanced than these, so if there were any way to reach into that history, Abram would at least have an idea that it was possible to have a child late on. Some of the children listed in Abram's genealogy saw their grandparents in the third and fourth generations. But whoever heard of someone coming into a foreign land only to own the whole country? Where would one look to find precedent for that?

Most decisions have to be made with incomplete information. The key is not to let this paralyse or take you into procrastination mode. Some decisions demand haste, and others come in situations that allow you some time to manoeuvre. At other times, not deciding or not doing anything *is the* decision. Each decision point has its context, so the best thing you can do is figure out each context's elements at the moment. Like being angry or irritable at home because of something that happened at work (and vice versa) is not okay, transplanting elements from one decision to another makes poor decisions. A few well-placed questions can help you take on a new perspective and arm you as much as you can be armed before acting.

What assumptions have I made about the situation or problem?

Assumptions are ubiquitous, a heuristic the brain adopts to make things go faster. After all, life is to be lived, not studied. While the constant advice to live mindfully is valid (mindful listening, eating, in stressful situations, at work.), your life would pass you by if you were an observer in all these situations. So, your brain works more like a predictive processor. It picks up environmental cues and does some quick calculations.

Have we been here before? If yes, what happened the last time? What shall we do differently if that outcome wasn't good this time? If not, what's the closest experience you have had, the ditto? If absolutely nothing resembles this, are there any stories in memory that somebody else might have told of something familiar or perhaps from a movie or a book? All of this (and more!)

is to give you a head start, especially if flight might be a reasonable choice. That is why you will feel your heart rate increase, start to sweat or just get clammy in tense situations. The thing is, the brain takes the anticipation of a 100-meter sprint and checking your investments as the same thing. It considers physical, emotional and psychological decisions using the same framework. Whatever the brain comes up with from this process generates a narrative, directs your focus, prepares the body, and emotions are attached to it all. In one word: assumptions.

In asking, "How shall I know I will inherit it (the land)," Abram said he wasn't so sure. He wanted some evidence, collateral, something to hold on to to be sure God's answer wasn't just a bunch of words. In reading the rest of the chapter, we know God gave him an answer. But God didn't have to go to the lengths He did. To Mary, the angel Gabriel simply answered. (Luke 1:35) Zachariah, on the other hand, was mute for at least nine months "because you did not believe my words." (Luke 1:18)

To avoid Abram's error (Was the "Know certainly that your descendants will be strangers in a land that is not theirs and will serve them, and they will afflict them four hundred years" punishment like Zachariah's case? Genesis 15:13), two questions may be helpful: what doesn't make sense here? What is so apparent here that I am not giving it the attention it deserves?

The obvious and the unusual

Abram did know how he could be sure he would inherit the land. He could know for sure because the same God who was promising him the land was the same God who promised him a child in his old age, and he believed. That is the contrast between having a child when you and your barren wife are advanced in years and inheriting the land; the latter seemed the easier. It simply doesn't make sense that he would immediately believe one promise and then ask for evidence for the next one. So while it is normal to be sure-footed in one area of faith and stumble in another, it seems worth considering that God is the over both areas. If you can trust Him for one thing, trust Him for the other.

An everyday application of the two questions may be in the disagreements that crop up at home. Just as an example, your significant other or perhaps another immediate family member is someone who loves you. Take that as a given, especially if the relationship dynamics are generally good. But then, they say or do something, and you feel hurt. Without realising it, your response doesn't depend on this given but a couple of substitute ones: they did it on purpose, and what you feel is because of *them*. It doesn't make sense that someone who loves you sat down and devised a plan they knew would cause you to lose trust in him. Someone who cares about you would not intentionally erect a wall between you and them, however temporary that may be. Yet, this is how you will respond.

The situation or the behaviour is the adversary, not the other person. The more reasonable approach, which is guaranteed to mend bridges rather than destroy them, is to see things from the original standpoint. This person loves me. From that point of view, they can be a collaborator. Together, you can find a solution to the problem. Instead of accusing the person of malevolence, employ curiosity. What did he intend if he *did not* say or do whatever they intended to hurt you? How can you let him know the thing he hoped for is appreciated, but perhaps the delivery method could be different next time? Can you give him the benefit of the doubt?

Expert assumptions

The Pharisees and Sadducees of Jesus' day held office in the leadership concerning religious matters. Being among that elite group was a career path. Their daily practice was studying the law and the prophets, learning, debating, interpreting, and building on the oral traditions of the rabbis who had gone before them. These entrenched the basic assumptions of their contemporaries and their teachers before them into their worldview. But as they became more experienced, they became increasingly blind to God's new things. He came to live among them, and they didn't recognise Him.

The expert is someone who has a superior and more nuanced way of seeing things in a specific area. They are familiar with its rules and laws and know how things behave in that domain. The cost of this expertise is that they often dismiss the things that fall outside that strict set of patterns. Kings inherit their positions as kingdoms pass from father to son. Would the King of kings be born in a stable? Though they had studied the prophecies for centuries, they missed His arrival. The Chief Priests and the scribes confirmed the legitimacy of the magi's search and told them where to go. And yet, no expert scholars were worshipping that night. In the first moments of Jesus's life, animals and poor, uneducated shepherds crowded His view as he experienced the world He had created with a baby's eyes. There were no expert scholars there.

As He ministered to the populace, they felt that Jesus fulfilled so many of the prophecies. "Could this be the Christ," they asked amongst themselves. (John 4:29) Yet the experts, fixated on their expectations, saw only those things that disproved His identity. How could the Messiah come from a depraved place like Nazareth? How could the Lawgiver, who declared adultery and fornication as sin, be a child conceived in iniquity and born out of wedlock? (John 8:41b) They missed God because, when He came, He didn't fit into their box of assumptions, predictions and expectations. Because the experts had their frame of reference and He didn't fit into it, they rejected and crucified the Lord of glory. (1 Corinthians 2:8)

In whatever you are dealing with, you will also miss the

idiosyncrasies and the things that a less experienced mind will notice. That will be until you make a habit of questioning the basic assumptions and risk looking dumb because of those questions. Toddlers universally respond to everything with curiosity, with a why question. Rediscover that curiosity.

How can I make this simpler?

Jesus said the law and the prophets—Genesis to Malachi and even those prophecies that speak of His second coming—could be summed up in *two commandments.* "You shall love the LORD your God with all your heart, with all your soul, and with all your mind. 'This is the first and great commandment. And the second is like it: You shall love your neighbour as yourself.'" (Matthew 22:37-39). If Jesus could summate the law of Moses, the totality of Exodus, Leviticus and Deuteronomy into two sentences, nothing need be as complicated as it might look at first. Simple things are elegant, but we often prefer the more complex as if they make us look intelligent. Unnecessarily complex things can be confusing, leading to more mistakes in decision-making.

Is it possible to have too much information? How many pieces of information do you need to feel confident you can make a decision? How many are enough?

In 1974, psychologist Paul Slovic1 evaluated the effect of information on decision-making in what has become a classic experiment. He gathered eight-horse handicappers, all seasoned professionals who made their livings solely on their gambling skills. How well could they predict the winners in forty horse races in four consecutive rounds?

Slovic gave each gambler any five pieces of information he wanted on each horse in the first round. He also asked each handicapper how confident he was in his prediction. In round one, with just five pieces of information, the handicappers were seventeen percent accurate with a confidence level of nineteen percent. In the second round, Slovic doubled the pieces of information. He gave them up to twenty and forty pieces of information in the third and fourth rounds, respectively. The extra pieces of information made them more confident. By the time they had all thirty-five additional data points, their confidence level was thirty-four percent. Surprisingly, their accuracy did not improve beyond seventeen percent. The additional information did not make them any better at their task, but they felt much more confident in their picks. They made bigger bets but also set themselves up for more significant losses.

The researchers concluded that other information only feeds *confirmation bias beyond a certain basic amount.* The data is only good when it makes us feel better about what we've already decided. If it conflicts with that assessment or conclusion, we conveniently ignore or dismiss it.

So, while effective decision-making demands that you collect different opinions and viewpoints, trying to project outcomes and influences, the world is far too complex to grasp. The results of Slovic's experiment are generalisable, and that suggests you need less information than you think to make good decisions. Less evidence. The challenge, therefore, is not so much looking for more evidence. Instead, it is to ask, what if I could only subtract to solve problems?

"If you had faith the size of a mustard seed, you could say to this mountain, "Move from here to there, and it will."" (Matthew 17:20) Who would have thought a man could move a mountain? And to do it, according to Jesus, would to a lot less than you think. To heal your relationships will take less than you think. Getting your business going for it to be profitable and make a significant contribution to society and your colleagues' lives will take less than you imagine. Deciding to follow Jesus, to answer His call, will not be as hard as you think. Be on the lookout for more straightforward solutions. They are the most effective.

↑ What if I did the opposite?

Most of the things we do and how we go about them come down to how it's always been done. In general, those assumptions that made sense to our teachers dictate how we approach life. There are some things that you cannot do any other way, but investigation suggests that list is smaller than you might think.

Take teaching. When Jesus taught, "The people were astonished at His teaching, for He taught them as one having authority, and not as the scribes." The Jews marvelled at Jesus, however, saying, "How does this Man know letters, having never studied?" (Matthew 7:28-29) He was, of course, very well versed in the Scriptures. He hadn't gone to any of their schools or been a disciple of one of the teachers they recognised. Like Jesus, you don't need a degree to become a teacher. Except for Paul, the gospel Jesus brought was borne out of Israel to the end of the earth by unqualified teachers: fishermen, tax collectors and the "unlearned" of the day. This is also God's approach in the Old Testament. God did much of His work through people who were so under-qualified that He had to convince them they could do the job.

Doing the opposite of what you have always done (or what other people are doing) stems mainly from two well-rehearsed ideas. If you do what you have always done, you will get the same results you've always been getting. This observation has spawned the opposite statement, "It is insane to do the same thing repeatedly and expect different results." If you are content to have a life below the highest God has for you, you can do more of what you have been doing. Even for a brief time, doing the opposite will radically change your life. Be the first to say hi when you meet people and do it with enthusiasm. Be the first to help when you see someone in need. Pray for others more than you pray for yourself. When you give, do so extravagantly, rather than calculating how much you will have left before you do. Be too kind and too merciful because there is no such thing. These are suggestions based on Jesus' teaching to turn the other cheek, go the extra mile and don't hold back when someone would borrow from you. The beatitudes are a call for doing the opposite, for being "perfect as your Father in heaven is perfect" rather than using the standards set by other people, cultures and society. (Matthew 4:18)

The second well-rehearsed idea is from Mark Twain: "If you even find yourself in the majority, it is time to take a moment and reflect." The typical path, the wide one, the route that everyone else takes, is not the one that leads to God's best. Take the road less travelled, and embrace the possibility that you may have to create your path. After all, you are uniquely created and qualified for your specific task. Your road won't look like anyone else's.

13

◆━━━○━━━▶

WHEN BAD IDEAS SEEM GOOD

O ne of the best decisions you can make is to do nothing. Often waiting is better than rushing into action. But how do you know when that is the best course?

⏐ The Cost of Doing Surgery

Everything we have learned about surgically intervening inside of a body, stabilizing the vitals and getting people on the road to recovery is a gift from God. Yet, even if it saves a life, every operation also traumatizes the body. Whatever needed to be removed or put back together, getting to it typically involves cutting some things that were intact. The more invasive the surgery, the greater the likelihood that doctors will use general anaesthetic over local. However professionally managed, the introduction of foreign gaseous compounds will force the body's immune agents into action.

Latent pain is an example of the cost of doing surgery. Latent pain is when a body part is injured, but there is a delay in when you feel the pain. While most studies measure pain months after surgery, one unusual design looked into the days immediately after a procedure. Researchers asked people who had had total hip replacements to rate their pain four times a day for the first four weeks. They found that the pain intensity decreased post-surgery, as you might expect. However, on average, it peaked again on the ninth day, almost to the same levels as it was just after! These higher intensities lasted three days before the pain eased off again.1 When the injury is to a nerve, as might happen during a surgical procedure, the pain might peak about a fortnight later.

The typical response to this increase in pain is to increase the medication. Total hip replacements are serious surgeries, and candidates benefit from them. Surgery, however, can bring about some unintended results like this resurgence in pain and the possibility of drug dependence as people try to manage it.

The Australian Rheumatology Association encourages doctors to discuss alternatives to surgery, such as exercise therapy, with their patients. As reported in 2018,

"For the first time, the peak body for rheumatologists has publicly urged doctors to avoid arthroscopic knee surgery, which can involve washing out the joint or cleaning up the lining, for patients with osteoarthritis, especially if they're over 50.

A growing body of research has shown the costly surgery is at best a placebo and, at worst, downright harmful, placing patients at increased risk of bleeding inside the joint and blood clots and exposing them to surgical risks such as infections and death."2

All of this considered, just because a surgeon can operate doesn't mean she should. There are often conservative approaches that will do the job credibly. Exercise therapy can be very effective for those with rheumatoid arthritis, those who have been the ideal candidates for these surgeries.

Similarly, there are many situations where the best thing you can do is hold off on any action. Resist that action bias, the deep urge to *do something*. Most of all, resist pressure from outside influences that will want to move you for their agendas. The trick is identifying when to respond with quietness and confidence.

Now Sarai, Abram's wife, had borne him no children. And she had an Egyptian maidservant whose name was Hagar. So Sarai said to Abram, "See now, the LORD has restrained me from bearing children. Please, go in to my maid; perhaps I shall obtain children by her." And Abram heeded the voice of Sarai.

Then Sarai, Abram's wife, took Hagar, her maid, the Egyptian, and gave her to her husband Abram to be his wife after Abram had dwelt ten years in the land of Canaan. So he went into Hagar, and she conceived. And when she saw that she had conceived, her mistress became despised in her eyes. Then Sarai said to Abram, "My wrong be upon you! I gave my maid into your embrace, and when she saw that she had conceived, I became despised in her eyes. The LORD judge between you and me."

So Abram said to Sarai, "Indeed, your maid is in your hand; do to her as you please." And when Sarai dealt harshly with her, she fled from her presence. (Genesis 16:1-6)

For Your Husband

There are some things to note here that set up a look at the man Abram from a light we don't often consider. First, the record begins with a statement that reflects Sarai's belief, quite possibly an extension of the views of their culture. *Abram's wife had borne him no children.* A detour to the beginning will be most instructive. Adam's aloneness was the only thing in all of creation that was "not good." (Genesis 2:18-25)

The defining quality of God's plan to resolve that blemish was "comparability." What God would create would be suitable, a complement, just right, a counterpart, a companion who corresponds to him. He made a woman. As a helper, her task was to provide the type of companionship Adam could not get from the animals. She would share in his having dominion over the fish, birds, livestock, wild animals and every creeping thing. God created her to help her husband with those parts that he could not do by himself, most notably being fruitful and multiplying. To do all this, she had to have certain qualities. Like Adam, Eve had to have intellect, the capacity to think and reason, to feel, hope and dream. She had wisdom, ambition, passion, courage, her own dreams and the drive to achieve them. Only then could she understand Adam and be a suitable helpmate. When they came together, however, she was to submit to him. God gave to her almost everything He gave to Adam. Those things He didn't give her, He gave her the capacity to complement her companion who did. The fall did not change this- when God said, "Your desire shall be for your husband, and he shall rule over you." (Genesis 3:16b) It is as much a word to direct her (prone to wonder) attention as a command.

This setting sheds light on the goings-on recorded in the Abram, Sarai and Hagar saga. Women have long defined themselves by their ability to bear children, a role critical to fulfilling the command to multiply and fill the earth. However, the Bible gives no sign of the primacy of this part of who they are. In other words, a woman is not less of a woman if she cannot or has not borne a child. The primary calling for a married woman is to be a companion for her husband. It was not that every other creature had offspring while Adam could not that God said was "not good." He was alone with no one to talk and laugh with, no one to share in the marvel of all that God had created. Sarai, however, had her desires for a child far more than she had for her husband. Abram is not blameless in this; we know he shared that deep desire. The error lies in the desperation that had overcome them both, so a terrible idea seemed promising.

Marriage required consummation, so their inability to have children had been known for a long time. If Abram's sole desire in marrying her was to have children, he could have taken another wife. The general practice in their day would not frown on that decision. There seemed to be no struggle with the idea of having multiple wives when Laban tricked Jacob into having Leah instead of Rachel.3 This is all the more significant because all of this happened amongst Abram's relatives back in Mesopotamia, from where God called Abram in the first place. (Genesis 29:27-28) This same source also confirms what Sarai proposes—having children by or through one's maid was also a common practice. Yet, Abram had chosen not to exercise any of those options. He valued their relationship so much as to not complicate it by bringing another woman into their lives, even if that meant he missed out on the chance to have children. Doing so would have allowed him to get what he wanted. It would only serve to remind his beloved wife of what *she* couldn't have. Though they shared this hope, this dream, how Sarai saw the situation and the plan she hatched to deal with it brought this issue about.

If she had considered what bringing another woman into their lives would have done to them, she probably would not have suggested Abram take Hagar as a wife. More importantly, if she did not define herself by whether she had given Abram children or not, but by every other quality she brought to their relationship, things might have turned out differently. Sarai focused on what she didn't have, and it consumed her. As it did, she knew she had to compromise, but she did not classify it correctly. You cannot undo putting another woman in your husband's bed any more than you can cleave a baby in half then put it back together. Nor can you have a baby the way Sarai imagined and not have to deal with his mother or pretend she doesn't exist. But Sarai was engulfed by her obsession until an idea she would not have entertained otherwise suddenly made sense. Bringing another woman into their marriage was suddenly a viable option. Untampered by desperation, Sarai would have seen that Abram himself had not chosen to go that way, even if the customary practice would have probably allowed it.

It would be harsh to judge them for everything, given we have the benefit of reading the story to its end, and they didn't. However absurd it seems to us when we read it, this plan was a potential solution, though it brought its own problems. In retrospect, Sarai would probably confess this was not the best idea. It was indeed a case where they could have waited. After all, God had called them from Mesopotamia to Canaan and given them the land. If there was evidence that *some* part of that promise was happening, they could trust that part of the promise about Abram's seed would also happen, even if they couldn't see how.

As a fundamental view, when there are many unknowns before you, it is helpful to focus on what you *do* know. You know God is faithful, and He keeps His word. He is always on time. If you are waiting on an answer, His intervention, or some other promise that seems to be taking too long, you can focus on what you know: just as Jesus came in the fulness of time, He will come through for you with the level of precision.

A lack of focus or redirection of it engendered this problem. When Sarai focused on a child more than her husband, she lost her way. When they focused on their need and planned how to bring that about, rather than focusing on the truth that their most profound desire was from God, they obscured their own path.

1. Sarai said, "The Lord has restrained me." If she were sure it was His specific action to hold her from having children, it would only make sense to go back to Him. If He had said no, then like Balaam, it was best to leave that path closed, lest she found out the Angel of the LORD was standing in the way with His sword drawn in his hand. (Genesis 27:43) It seems more like platitude when we hear it, but it is for our good that God closes the doors He closes. The "cherubim placed east of the garden of Eden and the flaming sword, which turned every way" was not placed there because God wanted to be cruel, letting them see the

garden but never entering. (Numbers 22:31) They guarded "the way to the tree of life." (Genesis 3:24)

Adam and Eve had been free to eat of it before for eternal life way theirs already. Eating that fruit after they had sinned would perpetuate sin for all eternity. The consequences for us when we insist on having relationships: business or personal, with those God has considered out of bounds, may not have eternal ramifications, but they will be costly somehow.

So how do you know when it's best to do nothing?

Listen. Listening is not just about being quiet; it is also about being present in the moment. As a believer, you benefit from serving an omniscient, omnipotent and benevolent Father. His delight is to speak to His child, help, deliver, and lift you up. Being present in the moment means being tuned to what He is doing in you, through you and for you. The path, as Abram shows, is not a linear one. He will lead you to green pastures, and you will dwell in the house of the Lord, but the journey doesn't end without a valley. It will pass through the shadow of death. He knows where you are in your journey, and He knows which way He is leading. Your only assignment is to walk before Him and listen.

14

WALK BEFORE ME

"When Abram was ninety-nine years old, the LORD appeared to Abram and said to him, "I am Almighty God; walk before Me and be blameless. And I will make My covenant between Me and you, and will multiply you exceedingly" (Genesis 17:1-2).

"Walk before Me and be perfect. Be blameless." This is the report we have of Enoch, (Genesis 5:24), Noah (Genesis 6:9) and Job (Job 1:1), and God calls Abraham to the same. Above all things, the calling of God is a call to holiness, to *be with Him.* (Matthew 5:48) If a holy God, wholly other, separate from sinners, calls you, you too must be separated, elevated and made different.

"Walk before Me" is an invitation into His presence, up to His level. It is a call to His standard, plan, strength, view, and expectations. His calling is also His guarantee that His command is not beyond you. If He has said it to you, He has simultaneously empowered, equipped and blessed you with whatever you need to finish the task. (Isaiah 55:11)

Because "Walk before Me and be blameless" is a command, both an enabling and an expectation. We often throw around the 'in my own strength' phrase to excuse ourselves from living up to God's high calling. It's a convenient statement because it is true in part. In time, the corruptible will put on the incorruptible, and the mortal will put on immortality, but only *after* the trumpet sounds. Yet, the Bible suggests a level of soundness, blamelessness, righteousness, and holiness that is the standard on *this side of that trumpet*. That standard is clear, once again, early in the story of humanity. For now, we can coast below the bar because it is unrealistic.

Rule over it

Genesis 4:6-7 is full of emotional intelligence elements, a critical factor in effective decision making and leadership. "So the LORD said to Cain, "Why are you angry? And why has your countenance fallen? If you do well, will you not be accepted? And if you do not do well, sin lies at the door. And its desire is for you, but you should rule over it.""

➤ Many believers have written off the idea of mindfulness because it has, in modernity, become synonymous with meditation and spiritual thinking that don't always align with the way of Christ. Mindfulness, however, is nothing more than being aware of what you are thinking and feeling. The Lord's questions show that He is aware of our emotions and that they matter. In this passage, the LORD not only acknowledges and addresses emotions, but He also asks Cain to put his finger on *why* he was feeling that way.

➤ "If you do well, will you not be accepted?" (Verse 7a) Emotions influence our behaviour and vice versa. Cain was upset because of how his offering was received. The proper response would have been to understand why and seize the opportunity "to do well" the next time. He was guaranteed to be accepted. Yet, his injured pride led him to see his brother as the aggressor and a problem that needed to be eliminated because he could not slow down enough to think this through.

➤ "Sin lies at the door, and its desire is for you, but you should rule over it." (Verse 7b) This statement is all-important. Sin, in the Lord's view, is not inevitable. It is outside, and no matter how great "its desire is for you," it cannot just burst in uninvited. As other translators have said, you must subdue it and be its master. Have dominion over it. What the Lord explains suggests sin only comes if "you refuse to do what is right." In other words, though He did not accept Cain's offering, the Lord did not consider it a sin. The Lord's questions invite introspection, and if Cain learned why he was angry, he would understand his posture and attitude (the fallen countenance). He would realize he was upset because the Lord had no respect for him or his offering, but that respect and acceptance were still available if he made the necessary adjustments.

The space in which we slow down enough to consider our emotions and our thoughts is the space in which the Holy Spirit works. The book of Psalms is replete with meditative, mindfulness-based questions. The contemplative pause is when the Spirit will point out the way you should go. During that reflection, He will highlight the word hidden in your heart, and if you heed it, it will keep sin at bay. "I have hidden your word in my heart that I might not sin against You." (Psalm 119:11)

Nobody has ever suffered from taking a step back to consider if he is "in the faith." You can probably think back to when you were caught up in the heat of the moment and did whatever seemed right at the time. If you dare to think deeply about those situations, you will also realize that there was a still small voice in that exact moment trying to steer you aright, but you ignored it. Inevitably, that ended up being something you regretted afterwards. "If you refuse to do what is right, then watch out! Sin is crouching at the door, eager to control you."

Sin waits to enter if you refuse to do well, to listen to My instructions, but you *must* master, dominate and rule [over] it. How? The power of the Holy Spirit lives within everyone who believes in the Son of God. He is an ever-present help today as He was with Cain. The sequence of events is poignant. The God who has seen the end from the beginning calls Cain to consider what he is feeling, why and how he can change *before* Cain does anything. The sin—the murder of his brother—only came when he refused to be mindful of what was happening inside him. That refusal opened the door. The crouching sin entered and dominated him.

The voice that declared the Father was well pleased with Jesus came before Jesus went into the desert. After forty days, during which He disciplined His mind, body and spirit, there was much that would have made Him more comfortable. Jesus had the power to turn the stones into bread, but He resisted, just as He resisted the allure of many kingdoms or angelic intervention to save His life. The words of Scripture were His repost. By sticking to those words and doing nothing else, He overcame.

The same will be true for you. Blamelessness is not about the hereafter. Righteousness is not reserved for when Jesus comes. Perfection of character is not only for when death has lost its sting and grave its victory. It is the standard of the here and now. It is the descriptor of every man and woman who has received Jesus and the right to be a child of God.

All you have to do is slow things down. Discipline yourself. Resist the urge to act on your first impulse, even your second. When you create time and space for the Holy Spirit to speak into your situation, you will always give yourself the chance to make a better decision.

15

ON HIS FACE

"Then Abram fell on his face, and God talked with him" (Genesis 17:3).

Picture going on all fours, then going even lower. Sitting on your haunches, put your hands and your face down. Your back is exposed. You have no protection. Expose your spinal cord and all the nerves that come from it. All the while, your face is on the ground. You can't see anything, and your hands are on the floor, covering neither your neck nor your head. This is a position of vulnerability.

It may be that God had intended to speak with Abraham about the covenant when He started the conversation. He was probably going to change his name regardless. Yet, the Bible goes through the trouble of describing this posture and interrupts the record of God's words, making it highly significant. Abraham fell on his face, not responding to something God had done, but due to who was talking to him. The almighty God was speaking, and that was sufficient.

There is nothing more important than the ability to distinguish the voice of God from the noise, to know for yourself that you are in His presence and He is speaking to you. What God has to say takes precedence over everything: opinions, feelings, wants, likes and preferences. This is the "fear of the Lord," to humble yourself before the mighty hand of God. Humility is about vulnerability and surrender. It is recognizing God, appreciating the weight of who He is, the power of His Word, and subordinating yourself to Him.

Think of Jesus in the garden. (Luke 22:39) As He suffered under the weight of the world's sin, He was clearly fully man. The total weight of the task ahead of Him became clear. Though He knew that it was necessary and He alone could do it, His body and mind wanted nothing to do with it. Yet, whatever He felt, He brought Himself low. The Father was God over Jesus's triumphs, and He was God over His greatest fears. "Let this cup pass from Me" is the recognition even the things that happened in His darkest hour were in the Father's hand. (Luke 22:42) Jesus knew God could turn anything in any direction He wanted; being His Son, He could pour Himself out before Him. To call the Almighty "Father" is to have freedom and privilege you won't find anywhere else. Who else can you be so vulnerable that you can be open about your deepest fears and confess your struggles and weaknesses without judgement or mockery?

"Nevertheless, not my will but yours be done", is saying; regardless of what I think or how I feel, I trust God to make the best decision. (Luke 22:42) The best thing for Him was that Jesus stayed on the path He was on. He had to drink the cup. It was *mainly* because Jesus surrendered to the Father's will that an angel came to strengthen Him. If you bring yourself to be vulnerable before the Father, you have the promise that He will hear you. Some things God intends for His glory and our benefit, so He will choose not to change or take away. He will, however, supply the strength we need to go through it.

One of the keys to better decision-making is committing to one decision that covers all else. Remember, effectiveness in what your calling comes when you reduce the number of decisions you must make by deciding on their hedgehog concept. No matter how attractive, everything beyond that is a "no." Humility, in this context, is a position, an outlook and an action. The one decision that directs them all is deference to God. The Almighty declared He has thoughts and ways of doing things, as far from yours as heaven is from the earth and the east from the west. If this is always the case (and it is), then every situation has another perspective, and every task has another approach. Effective decisions are only those that last after you fall on your face and approach God with a sincere "nevertheless, not my will but Yours." Talking with God about the specifics of your situation is different from being in a relationship in general. Don't assume God's agreement or involvement in your affairs. Engage Him in them.

David never forgot that God had brought him up keeping the sheep. When he became king, he was not content to live in a cedar palace while God's ark lived "inside tent curtains." He had it in his heart to build something even more illustrious for the ark than for himself. It was such a noble plan that the prophet Nathan, one whose job was literally to speak of God, gave his blessing on the project. "The Lord is with you," he told David. But it happened that night that the word of the LORD came to Nathan, saying, "Go and tell My servant David, 'Thus says the LORD: "Would you build a house for Me to dwell in?" (2 Samuel 7:1-17) David's sword had spilt too much blood, and while the plan was a real show of humility, David was not going to be the one to build it. God accepted the gift, loved the heart behind it, but He had other ideas on how the building would come to stand. If a prophet could feel an idea would surely have God's blessing only for the Lord to say, "I want that done differently," you cannot take it for granted that an idea will have His go ahead. The bigger the decision, the greater the need to tune into His voice and make sure you are aligned. Some things will only be able to see when you find the courage to set aside your convictions and strongest desires and fall on your face before God.

Humility in Action

"Let this mind be in you which was also in Christ Jesus, who, being in the form of God, did not consider it robbery to be equal with God, but made Himself of no reputation, taking the form of a bondservant, and coming in the likeness of men. And being found in appearance as a man, He humbled Himself and became obedient to the point of death, even the death of the cross." (Philippians 2:5-8)

No biblical conversation on humility would be complete without this scripture. It is about going from theory to practice. The answer to that ubiquitous Christian question is, what does this look like? Humility is not a checklist. Yet, some things, like a shadow, are always observable when you think of someone who is genuinely humble.

> **Disregard self.** Jesus was equal with God. (John 1:1-4) John's gospel begins with a declaration of such. There would be rights, privileges and dues associated with that; yet, for God's great plan, He set all of that aside. He was King and Lord but made Himself of a no reputation.

> The simplest and most observable form of this is in acknowledging others. Humble people go to great lengths to shine the limelight on friends, family and others who have helped them. Their speeches are full of "we" as they share the credit for any accomplishments with all those people.

> **Service.** It was for love He had for His creation that Jesus humbled Himself to death on a cross. To save them, He would have to serve them. He committed to that cause to the point of washing their feet. Humble people understand that the reason to which they pledge their service will not be realized by them alone. In their work, investment

in others is visible. They mentor, volunteer, teach and prepare others because they know their cause will outlast them. They will need others to complete the mission, and as such, they consider the readiness of the next generation one of their primary aims. After washing His disciples' feet, Jesus talked about what He was doing as an example for them. Go and do likewise. (John 13:1-15)

> **Listening.** Jesus was unusual in several ways as a teacher. He associated with women, tax collectors, Pharisees and the leprous. Most remarkable, however, was that Jesus even had time for children. (Mark 10:13-16) Modern systems with the involvement of teachers, coaches, mentors and tutors- are set up so you believe your attention is only for those who are smarter or better than you somehow. It takes some humility to have time to spare for children, subordinates, or anyone else who doesn't seem they can teach you something. Humble people believe everyone is valuable, that each person's experiences and views are worthy of consideration. As such, they approach life with a deep curiosity. They are genuinely interested in the thoughts other people have. They know nobody has a monopoly on promising ideas, so they are always on alert, never knowing where or when inspiration might come. When they talk to others, they spend more time asking questions and listening than they do telling them what to do.

All of these are only possible because humility comes from high self-esteem. Jesus knew who He was, that He was going to the Father, and that, as He washed His disciples's feet, He was where He needed to be to carry out His mission.

The answers to who, where, and what, for the believer, are only found when you fall on your face before God.

16

GENEROSITY IS GODLIKENESS

Please, let a little water be brought, and wash your feet, and rest yourselves under the tree. And I will bring a morsel of bread that you may refresh your hearts. So Abraham hurried into the tent to Sarah and said, "Quickly, make ready three measures of fine meal; knead it and make cakes." And Abraham ran to the herd, took a tender and good calf, gave it to a young man, and he hastened to prepare it. So he took butter and milk and the calf which he had prepared, and set it before them. (Genesis 18:4-8)

Generosity is one of the elements of God's character that is conspicuous in the Bible. The central theme of the New Testament is that God expressed His loving by His generosity. Giving is a form of blamelessness, which humanity can partake in and be like Him. It certainly was a regular part of Abram's life and with his name changed to Abraham, that stayed the same. A Jewish tradition suggests that Abraham constantly had guests in his home and that his large tent had doorways facing each of the four approaching roads. He was looking for people to invite into his home. As a result, another tradition says Abraham built a close circle of friends, numbering at least 20,000 souls.[1] Whatever the number, and the dividends paid to him because he unknowingly invited angels into his tent, the lesson is open for all to practice.

Abraham would undoubtedly fall in the class of the cheerful giver. He gave neither grudgingly nor of necessity. (2 Corinthians 9:7) In a beautiful illustration of empathy, Abraham asked himself what it would be like to be travelling in the heat without any provisions. In the heat of the day, some shade would be helpful, and some decent food would be very refreshing. It was not difficult for him to imagine their needs. After all, he had been a traveller himself. From a place of understanding, he acted to meet their needs.

As Abraham saw it, generosity was not only for people who would help him in the future. To be a cheerful giver is to give without the expectation of reciprocity. Abraham knew these guys had nothing with them, and as travellers, they did not have anything to give back to him. He wasn't approaching it as a trade or a business deal. He was aware that the flocks from which he plucked the kid, the butter and the cakes were only his because God gave them to Him.

Abraham didn't do the bare minimum. Overflowing with excitement, he persuaded the travellers to stay and eat: "If I have found favour in your sight, please"... "refresh your hearts." He abased himself before them: "inasmuch as you have done to your servant." (Genesis 18: 3-4) Compare what Abraham offered the travellers and what he did. He went beyond, and he did it without them having to ask, rationalize whether they would use or abuse the gift. Abraham was generous without calculating how much it would cost him to do it. It would be easy to say Abraham could afford to give as extravagantly as he did because he was wealthy. Remember that Jesus commended the widow who gave two mites. (Mark 12:41-44) The total amount was negligible, but she gave all she had in His estimation.

Generosity is not difficult. It comes down to whether you believe another human being is worth being served by you or not.

If you do, then you can risk your life to save another. That is why Jesus came. Or you can share a cup of water, share a meal or open your home. Service has a dual meaning, one doing something as if you were someone's servant and the other going to church for a prayer service. The word for both is *avodah*, which carries a third meaning to work in Hebrew. By this word, there is a connection between work, worship and service. It is the reason Jesus said that whatever we do for the least of His, we do for Him. In a beautiful connection, *ahav*, meaning "I give," is one of the words for love.[2] To love God with all your heart, mind and soul, and love your neighbour as yourself is to give to them. It is to serve them. As Abraham did, your task is to learn how to relate to all people with the empathy, warmth, sincerity, kindness and interest that turns strangers into friends.

Abraham's ability to do so had everything to do with his and Sarah's pronouncement, the news they had waited a lifetime to receive. They were unprepared for it, having extended their hospitality with no expectation of getting anything back. "I will certainly return to you," the Lord promised. This time next year, you will have a son, and your age will not be a factor. (Genesis 18:10) Their ages would not be a factor, for nothing is too hard for the Lord. The Philippians text about humility explains what happened. To the depth that Jesus became flesh and blood, subject to temptation and humiliating death on the cross, God exalted Him above anything else. (Philippians 2:5-8) Because He had been willing to go so low, God lifted Him up to the highest. Because Abraham and Sarah had been willing to give, God gave back to them, and it was more than they had imagined.

"Give, and it will be given to you: good measure, pressed down, shaken together, and running over will be put into your bosom. For with the same measure that you use, it will be measured back to you." (Luke 6:38)

Service, particularly when giving up something of yours, is the fastest way to get what you want. The more you give, the more you'll receive because that is the law as God wrote it, just like He wrote the law of gravity. Moreover, anytime we practice generosity, we take part in and propagate the gospel. The good news is God *did* something to show His great love for the world, fallen though it is. He gave when He didn't have to. He could have destroyed it all as in the days of Noah and started again. It would have cost Him nothing. But since the beginning, when He first conceived the idea to create man, He loved us, and that love moved Him to sacrifice His only begotten Son.

Impact Big and Small

When Jesus came, His life was all about giving. He multiplied the bread and fish loaves, and the crowds ate. (Matthew 6:1-4) Within hours, they were hungry again. He raised people back to life, but they all eventually died. So too, those He restored health. The Father's gift in sending Jesus was the first and greatest act of generosity. Jesus's ministry gives a glimpse of what generosity is about: impact. That hunger, sickness and death followed Jesus' interventions do not diminish their necessity. When He used His power, it changed people's lives. None of them would have refused His help because those things would come again in the future. Often we hold back from service and other types of giving because we feel it won't have any impact or change anything. Giving someone who needs it a cup of water, a plate of food or some shelter makes all the difference.

There is another level of impact, one to which the Lord has called everyone.

We are still benefiting today from what Jesus did, and many others will after us. While He didn't necessarily set out to be remembered over two thousand years later, the impact of His actions and words have achieved that. The same is true of Moses, Martin Luther, Isaac Newton, Leonardo Da Vinci, Mother

Theresa, Albert Einstein, Martin Luther King Jr., Nelson Mandela and many others. These were not people who did what they did looking for glory. Their intention was not to become immortal in stories or statues. Instead, they all asked themselves the same questions: *what problem exists now that I can try to solve and be involved in reducing or eliminating? What question can I dedicate time, energy and resources to answer?* Once they found answers, they threw themselves into it. It is their unwavering commitment to these that keep us talking about them. We will continue to talk about them in the future because when they answered those questions, they didn't settle for trivial matters. They looked at global things, and in so doing, their actions began or contributed to something that continues after they were gone.

As you think about generosity, ask yourself, what am I passionate about? What big problem plagues the world today that I am uniquely gifted to tackle? Once you find it, your next question is, what is the smallest thing that I can do that can have an impact? Go and do that thing. And then the next, and the next and the one after that. It is in and out of the things we repeatedly do that we build and live our lives.

17

LOOKING FOR THE RIGHT

"Shall not the Judge of all the earth do right?" (Genesis 18:25). A consequence of the closer relationship between God and Abraham is the latter's boldness in how he approaches the Almighty. Since God declared to Abram, "I am your shield, your exceedingly great reward," we begin to read back and forth conversations rather than just hearing the words of God to him. Abram took advantage, asking Him, "What good are your blessings if I don't have a son?" (Genesis 15:1-2) Now, Abraham goes further.

"And the Lord said, 'Because the outcry against Sodom and Gomorrah is great, and because their sin is very grave, I will go down now and see whether they have done altogether according to the outcry against it that has come to Me; and if not, I will know.'" (Genesis 18:20-21)

The implication is clear; if the outcry of Sodom and Gomorrah is as bad in person as it is from heaven, I will destroy it. Abraham thought of his nephew as soon as he heard that. Lot could not have forgotten what he had learned from him, and while Abraham could arm the servants of his own house to rescue Lot from the kings on earth, that approach would not work for the trouble heading for Sodom and Gomorrah now. It is poetic that the LORD decided to tell Abraham what he was going to do on the basis "that he may command his children and his household after him, that they keep the way of the Lord, to do righteousness and justice." (Genesis 18:19) It is to this same sense of justice that Abraham appeals.

"Shall not the Judge of all the earth do right?" (Genesis 18:22-33) is a call to assume there is something worth salvaging and to look for it. Not doing that would be *unlike* God. In Noah's time, the Lord could have wiped out all creation and started over, but He didn't. He found one who was righteous. (Genesis 6:9) Could God not do the same with Sodom and Gomorrah? What follows is a negotiation in which Abraham concedes that while there is sure to be something worth saving, there might not be much of it. The LORD agrees and says for whatever number of people Abraham sets (from 50 down to 10), He would spare the city for their sake. Would the city have been spared if He only five righteous people there? Abraham pleaded with the LORD not to be angry as they talked, and there is no indication He was, so perhaps Abraham could have continued to ask. Only three made it out alive, given Lot's wife and her well-known story, so it would not have mattered if Abraham had gone down to five people. The point is the freedom of speech Abraham found because of his relationship with God. He made his request known to God with both reverence and boldness.

Noteworthy in this exchange is the focus Abraham had. We are all almost experts at noticing the deficits, failures and shortcomings in other people. Unfortunately, some of us grew up in environments where people went to extreme lengths to point these out in us. As a result, so many people walk around highlighting the worst things about themselves. In engaging with Abraham, God confirmed the idea that even in the worst situation, there is some beauty, some worth, some righteousness that deserves attention. To destroy the righteous with the wicked is to wrap yourself up in all your deficits and assume there is nothing worth loving, saving, appreciating or celebrating. Whether it is weight, some standard of beauty, intelligence, or decisions we made in the past, our focus is on how far we have fallen from that imaginary gold standard.

Filters

We experience an estimated 19,200 moments in a day[1], and of those, "Scientists estimate that we remember only one in every 100 pieces of information we receive." Like the spam filters in our emails, the rest of that information is screened and filtered. It comes down to something that has 100 percent control over our attitude.[2] Whether through what others have done to us or repetition without awareness, we naturally point out what could be better. Whether we are aware of it or not, in pointing those out, we have magnified to people (and perhaps to ourselves) how they are not quite good enough, don't measure up, and never will. Our default filters highlight problems, errors, mistakes, faults, and flaws for many of us, so we unintentionally filter out success. It is, of course, essential to see these things. But if these are all we notice, then our world becomes full of nothing but errors, mistakes, and flaws.

"Do you think that I like to see wicked people die? says the Sovereign LORD. Of course not! I want them to turn from their wicked ways and live. Turn, turn from your evil ways! For why should you die, O house of Israel?'" (Ezekiel 18:23, 33:11) If the Judge of all the earth, who will do right, has a positive view and a yearning for even the most wicked to live, how much more should we? The conversation between God and Abraham is a chance to recognize that you can and must consciously choose where you direct your attention.

The New Testament echoes the same sentiment. Finally, brethren, whatever things are true, whatever things are noble, whatever things are just, whatever things are pure, whatever things are lovely, whatever things are of good report, if there is any virtue and if there is anything praiseworthy—meditate on these things. (Philippians 4:9)

The directive is to be selective in your thinking.

18

ASSUMPTIONS AND EMOTIONS

"And Abraham said, "Because I thought, surely the fear of God is not in this place, and they will kill me on account of my wife." (Genesis 20:11)

On either side of the birth of Isaac are two surprising records.

Assumptions

Abraham circumcised Isaac on the eighth day after his birth, "as God commanded him." These are the actions of a man who believes in God, trusts in Him and obeys Him. Circumcision was the covenant sign between him and God, showing Abraham's commitment to God.

Where was this Abraham in Gerar when he reverted to the "She is my sister" approach? (Genesis 20:2)

From his mouth, we learn he did this because he thought, "Surely the fear of God is not in this place, and they will kill me on account of my wife." (Genesis 20:11) He was afraid of what people who did not fear God would do to him. On the one hand, this is a suitable response. We expect believers to tell the truth, be faithful and kind, gracious, have faith, live without worry and anxiety. It would be somewhat naive to expect those same things from non-believers. After all, we do it because He who has saved us commands it and empowers us to live that way. On what grounds can we expect the non-believers to act that way?

However, to what degree should we let how the world's cultures influence our actions? Should we, citizens of a higher kingdom, allow the world to cause us to abandon our integrity?

Abraham leaned on the technicality that Sarah was his father's daughter but not his mother's, just like he did with Pharaoh in Egypt. Once again, he placed Sarah in an awkward position. He let his fear cause him to lie—based on an assumption. "I thought, surely the fear of God is not in this place." (Genesis 20:11) What made him think so?

Abraham made the mistake of thinking he was the only one, or one of the few, who believed in the one true God. He judged the people of Gerar on outward appearance and assumption rather than evidence. The Lord didn't have a conversation with Pharaoh about Sarah. He plagued his house. (Genesis 12:17) In contrast, God came to Abimelech in a dream and spoke with him at night. In response, Abimelech says, "Lord." Moreover, Abimelech challenges God, asking: "Will You slay a righteous nation also... In the integrity of my heart and innocence of my hands I have done this." (Genesis 20:5) These suggest, if not a relationship between them, an acknowledgement of who God is at the very least.

After the Lord had healed all affected, Abimelech chose not just to bless Abraham but also to keep him around. The connection to God through this prophet was something he wanted. Was the fear of the Lord in that place? It seems like it was. Even if it wasn't, the Lord had stepped into the situation with Pharaoh, showing He would be with Abraham wherever he went. Such evidence should have influenced Abraham's handling of this situation.

Your brain uses shortcuts to help you decide and act very

quickly. Among those shortcuts are generalizations, stereotypes, biases and assumptions. Most of these were knit into how you see life without your knowledge. Your experiences, those of your family, culture, and the media all come together, like wearing glasses or contacts. They influence what you see, and you are barely aware you have them on. Without an awareness of these, you will live your life on autopilot and repeat Abraham's mistake.

Affective Forecasting

Following the encounter with Abimelech, the story takes some significant leaps forward. The son of promise is born, and a dream of nearly a hundred years finally becomes a reality. Eight days later, they held a feast as Isaac was weaned. The overjoyed couple shared their joy with everyone. But it was not all joy.

One of the challenges of humanity is our constant awareness of the limitations around us. If you are not intentional about what you focus on, your default will be on the restrictions, deficiencies and what is lacking.

A father of two lovingly paying attention to one of his sons is automatically not paying attention to the other. The feast marked the crossing from one stage of life to another. Isaac would be a man inheriting his father's blessing in the blink of an eye. Preserving the status quo meant he would have less of what he could have if another child could claim part of that. Sarah "saw the son of Hagar the Egyptian, whom she had borne to Abraham scoffing." (Genesis 21:9) Was she seeing an older brother playing with his sibling? Was there something antagonistic in his air or something sinister in his voice? Was he rough with him? Whatever she saw, Sarah determined that there was no room for Ishmael.

"Therefore she said to Abraham, 'Cast out this bondwoman and her son; for the son of this bondwoman shall not be heir with my son, namely with Isaac.'" (Genesis 21:10)

What a change! When it was convenient, Ishmael was her son. He was how she would be "builded up," since she had not had a child. Yet now that the Lord allowed her to bear a son, she no longer cared for Ishmael even in her old age. To secure the blessing for her flesh and blood, she decided to get rid of Ishmael. And just like she had done the first time around, she put it on, Abraham.

Imagine what it was like for Abraham to hear her say that. Ishmael was his first-born son, his flesh and blood, a son who was only there because Sarah had suggested it. Sarah was ready to cast Ishmael aside shows that he and Hagar had just been a means to an end for her. But to Abraham, Ishmael was so special that he was concerned for his son even as God made him eternal promises and made them known. And Abraham said to God, "Oh, that Ishmael might live before You!" (Genesis 17:18) Though God had made it clear he intended to set up his covenant through Isaac, Abraham still circumcised Ishmael. He marked him as his child, as one of the people of God with whom the 'Possessor of heaven and earth' was in covenant.

So why, if Abram loved Ishmael so much, does he send him and his mother away with so little? Abraham "had sheep, oxen, male donkeys, male and female servants, female donkeys, and camels." (Genesis 12:16) The saga's conclusion with Abimelech reads: "Abimelech took sheep, oxen, and male and female servants, and gave them to Abraham; and he restored Sarah, his wife, to him. And Abimelech said, "See, my land is before you; dwell where it pleases you." Then to Sarah, he said, "Behold, I have given your brother a thousand pieces of silver." (Genesis 20:14-16) Abraham had separated from his nephew Lot because the sheer number of livestock he had was such that the land could not hold the two of them. Abraham armed three hundred and eighteen trained servants born in his own house to rescue Lot later. (Genesis 14:14)

From all of that, "Abraham rose early in the morning, and took bread and a skin of water; and putting it on her shoulder, he gave it and the boy to Hagar, and sent her away." (Genesis 21:14)

Could he not spare a sheep, a goat, a camel, a servant or two to make their fresh start, wherever they would end up a touch easier? With the land before him and permission to dwell where he pleased, could Abraham not afford a small acreage for his son and his mother to start a new life?

We have praised his generosity, so it couldn't have been because he was stingy. Abraham was troubled at Sarah's request (demand?), so it was likely not because he, too, was trying to save his inheritance for Isaac. Did Sarah have something to do with how much he gave them? Troubled as he was, Abraham sent them away because the Lord intervened. His response was not the reason for sending them away so poorly equipped? Despite this poor sending away, Ishmael returned when Abraham died and, together with Isaac, buried their father. (Genesis 25:9) He held no grudge.

Sarah's response to discomfiture was to get rid of the stressor. Ishmael was sent away, including once before he was even born! Sarah lacked the fortitude to take responsibility for her actions or decisions, but she also cared little about how others around her were doing if she was satisfied.

The subject in this chapter is the role of emotions in decision-making. Every choice you make has some feeling behind it. One way to interpret Daniel Kahneman's Prospect Theory[1] quadrants is that we are very illogical in our approach to decision-making. It is what we care about the most in each situation that directs whether we will lean one way or another. We will take more significant risks to avoid loss and do things that don't make logical or mathematical sense because we're hoping to have a feeling. Knowing these tendencies and other strategies the brain makes to arrive at decisions will help you identify them when you read and listen to other people's stories.

Psychologists have introduced the term affective forecasting[2] to describe some of the decisions in this story. It describes the way people make decisions hoping (and maybe somewhat like weather, predicting) that choice will make them feel good. Often, it is in a vain attempt to extend the way they feel when deciding on some endless future. In affective forecasting, somehow, we do not account for time. If you can think of when you noticed your new car smell was gone when the euphoria of moving into a new house waned, or perhaps the so-called honeymoon phase of a relationship ends. You notice the "routine"—these are examples of decisions made with affective forecasting at play.

Miswanting

Miswanting[3] is another psychological term for those things we focus on as we are affective forecasting. In short, the hope of projecting some (feeling of) present joy or excitement into the future creates a bias toward things or experiences, through the focusing illusion, to miswant and, therefore, overvalue things that will inevitably lose their initial appeal.

Sarah, as we saw, lost her focus and placed it on having a child more than on her husband. She thought a child, by any means necessary, would significantly improve her happiness. Whenever you make decisions from an "any means necessary" position, you are already subject to the focusing illusion, the psychological term for that habit of giving our attention to something so wholly that it dominates our worldview. When you focus on something, everything conspires to put it on a pedestal until it becomes the most crucial thing in the world. The truth, however, is that nothing in the world is as essential or as heavily weighted as you think it is when you are thinking about it. By holding it up, you see nothing else. I must have a child. Even if the Lord has stopped me from having one, I must have a child. With this level of focus and desperation, it is not surprising that Sarah couldn't see the flaws in the plan she hatched.

Time didn't improve this lack of awareness. Sarah wanted

to have a child through Hagar but on her terms. As soon as she didn't like how Hagar looked at her, she turned to Abraham and said, "Cast her out!" She wanted the baby; he could have done without his mother. Once he arrived, Ishmael was hers—that is what she had planned all along. Sarah may have been content then, but God intended to bless her and Abram with a child she would carry herself. That changed everything. After Isaac was born, Sarah no longer needed Ishmael, though he had been a source of joy and comfort to her for over ten years. She had had the benefit and blessing of calling herself a mother, but now, having had her baby, Hagar and Ishmael had no place in her home. Once again, she turned to Abraham and said, *Get rid of my problem for me.* In each case, Sarah was emotionally driven and spectacularly blind. She thought her solution would make her happy. The obvious flaws in her plan either didn't occur to her, or she thought she was immune to them.

The emotional attachments we naturally have to our ideas cause us to be unaware of when we behave like Sarah, though her errors are plain to see when reading the story. What is needed is an inventory of sorts. You probably have one or two relationships that are not as good as you would like them to be. To get them to that level, you'll need to ask some challenging questions. Humility and courage will beget better sleep and more pleasant meetings with those people in the future. Ask yourself, in those relationships, what have you done to contribute to the current problems? What emotions have driven you to behave this way with this person? Blindspot bias is almost always at play. You will see yourself as the victim or the only one who can see the truth in that situation. This avenue of thinking feeds your ego and stands in the way of what you want. Take some responsibility. Maybe you failed to be clear when you had that misunderstanding. You made some assumptions about what the other person said. Or perhaps you were so busy trying to make sure the person heard the point you were trying to make that you didn't think to acknowledge the hurt he expressed. Whatever it is, you have had a hand in how the current problem developed. Own it and take some steps to fix it.

You will also profit from trying to understand the situation from the other person's point of view. What do you think is driving the other person's behaviour? What is motivating him to act in these specific ways? What emotions is he trying to express? These questions reflect Jesus's command: do to others what you would want them to do for you. (Matthew 7:12) You want people to understand you; show that you understand them. If you want people to hear you out, first make every effort to make them feel they have been heard and understood.

19

❖———◇———➤

COVENANTAL CONVERSATION

"Then Abraham rebuked Abimelech because of a well of water which Abimelech's servants had seized. And Abimelech said, "I do not know who has done this thing; you did not tell me, nor had I heard of it until today." (Genesis 21:25-26 NKJV)

God's prescription for healing relationships and living harmoniously with others is to make the first to move. Be the one to build the bridge. That is precisely what Abraham did with Abimelech, albeit belatedly.

The seizing of the well had upset Abraham, but he had held onto it. He took the opportunity to address it when Abimelech and Pichol approached him to secure the future of their people. His grievance was that Abimelech's servants had seized a well Abraham had dug, and Abimelech had done nothing about it. The suggestion is that the king is responsible for the actions of his people. Abimelech, however, did not know what had happened or who had done it.

Moreover, he said to Abraham, "You did not tell me," suggesting the relationship between them was such that he could tell him anything. Why he asked, am I only hearing about this today? Perhaps he would have found the culprits and dealt with them accordingly had he known sooner. The language of the Bible suggests that from Abimelech's point of view, neither the rebuke nor the seven ewe lambs and the oxen were necessary. As a partner and friend, Abimelech expected Abraham to have told him rather than keep it to himself and feel slighted. Indeed, Abimelech did not come to make reparation. He was there with his agenda.

We often feel hurt by something said or done or an unfulfilled expectation about which the other has absolutely no idea. To avoid the unnecessary hurt, disappointment, and perhaps even the anger that comes from these one-sided affairs, the urging of the scripture here is to seek reconciliation early. As Jacob and Esau did, going for years with unresolved issues is not the way. We must go to a place of authenticity and vulnerability among friends and loved ones. The sooner we do it, the more productive we can be.

What would it take to have a relationship where you can be open and say how you feel without the fear of hurting the other? The Bible has the answer to that: perfect love. (1 John 4:18) Is there a better illustration of love than God's gift of His Son? Is there a more perfect love than the Man who laid down His life for His friends? What is the cross but a bridge to reunite us with God? He loves us with perfect love, and that lens explains much of what would otherwise be difficult to understand in some of Jesus's conduct. When He made a whip of chords and overturned the tables in the marketplace, He disciplined out of love. He chastised the son He loved when He said, 'Woe to you,' instead of a blessing. Jesus was making a point when thrice He asked Peter, 'Do you love me more than these,' and though it took Peter feeling hurt to get it across. In all of these instances and more, Jesus did what he did without worrying that they might misconstrue His meaning and run rather than turn to Him. What Jesus said and did among the people daily demonstrated His compassion. He trusted that those He was addressing knew how deeply He loved them at these difficult times. Indeed, He loved them that He corrected as He did, and there was no fear.

Fear involves torment. It has to do with punishment, with a sense of right and wrong. In close relationships, perhaps more prominent than issues of right and wrong are the feelings of being hurt or being safe. You might forget to compliment your spouse on an outfit or a job well-done. Or perhaps not express that you notice and appreciate the small things. It is neither right nor wrong in these cases, but when you yearn to be seen and affirmed, and that does not happen is not met, there could be feelings of hurt.

Empathy in Communication

The strength of any relationship depends on the quality of the communication. When you are talking, you need to speak with a level of self-awareness that shows you are communicating to improve the relationship. When you are listening, you need to be present. If people know you will hear them out, without interrupting, belittling or judging them, they will happily come to you and let you know what is going on with them at any given time. You will have to learn not to take things personally while figuring out how to express yourself without attacking the person you are talking to when it's your turn. Whenever there is an issue, always approach the conversation with a mindset of co-creating the solution. The person you are dealing with is not the problem-the matter between you is. Each of you will see it from your point of view. They will have their reality, and you will have yours. The more effort you can exert to appreciate things from the other person's position, the better. You don't have to agree with it or condone it; you have to be able to see it as they see it.

Jesus was like us in every way that matters. The Son of God was flesh and blood, born of a woman and needed to eat, drink, sleep. Most importantly, He lived in a depraved place and time both spiritually and politically, meaning he was not immune to temptation. By God's grace and power from heaven, He resisted temptation and lived a perfect life. "For in that He Himself has suffered, being tempted, He is able to aid those who are tempted." (Hebrews 2:18) For we do not have a High Priest who cannot sympathize with our weaknesses but was in all *points* tempted as *we are, yet* without sin. (Hebrews 4:15)

In other words, Jesus's pleas on our behalf as someone who has walked in our shoes and seen the world through our eyes. He does not make excuses for sin. He does not condone it. When He prays, "Father forgive them," and gives new mercies every morning, it is not because His experience as one of us makes Him more tolerant of evil. When He extends His grace, it is because the Holy One loves us with perfect love *at the same time* that He hates what we do. (Hebrews 1:9) His eyes are too pure to behold evil, but the sinner is the apple of His eye. (Habakkuk 1:13 and Deuteronomy 32:10) Can there be a better illustration of seeing the world as someone else sees it (and how they see themselves in that world), of hearing their point of view and understanding it without agreeing or taking it on yourself? Nothing less would do in God's plan to reconcile us with Himself, and nothing less will be enough in your relationships.

Emotional Intelligence

In other words, if you want to have more prosperous, more collaborative relationships, you must improve your self-awareness, largely considered the first pillar of emotional intelligence (EI).

When people have low EI, they will act oblivious to how others around them might feel. They spare no thought for how others' motivation, energy or confidence might be affected. These are the actions of excessively self-focused people. Contrast this with the conversation over this well. Though the patriarch felt Abimelech was wrong, he, Abraham, brought the sacrifice to make peace. The one who was hurt was the one who went out of his way to make things right. He took action, something that cost *him* because he wanted reconciliation. He effectively bought the well, though he had dug it himself.

Abraham's approach exemplifies the same principle that Jesus's life did.

God created humanity because He willed it. Everything He made from the first day to the fifth was in the exact order it needed to be so that the earth was inhabitable. On the sixth day, when He formed man in His own image, it was to begin a relationship. Like all of His covenants, we would benefit from the connection. God had the worship of the angels, and nature testifies to His glory. So it wasn't out of boredom or the need to have more worshippers. Worship exults God because He is worthy, but we get more out of it than He does. In Eden, the voice of the Lord came down, in the cool of the day, to speak with Adam and Eve. Their bond was intimate- God could have sent angels to deliver whatever information He wanted to give them, but He chose to come down. He gave them what was His- dominion, authority, leave to name the animals, and power to tend the garden. They could roam freely in their paradise and eat from whatever tree they wanted, except for one. All He wanted from them in return was their obedience. Their failure was a breach of trust, and it cost them everything. But God, the one hurt, disappointed and disrespected by what they had done, took steps to rescue the situation. He killed an animal and used its skin to cover Adam and Eve's nakedness, a foreshadowing of Jesus's blood that would dress us in His righteousness.

In short, the one who feels hurt has the power to make things right that the offender does not. But the Biblical prescription is costly. First and foremost is the issue of pride. We typically hold on to some righteous anger and wait for the offender to come and apologize. As Abimelech showed, sometimes the offender is none the wiser. Sometimes, the matter is generational, as it was between the Jews and the Samaritans. At other times, it is not even a matter of doing something but disappointed expectations. Whatever the case, God moved first to restore us; Abraham brought the animals, Jesus went to Samaria and then made the sacrifice. The cross is a timeless reminder that relationships are more important than any grievance, and you need to commit to taking the first step.

The Amygdaloid Night Watchman

Recall the concepts of PEA and NEA. Emotions are contagious whether you hold them back or express them. This peculiarity has led to the study of emotional dynamics in different contexts. Researchers can say negative emotions are more potent than positive emotions[2] though *how much* stronger they are is still under investigation. We know so far that when words and positive behaviour outnumber negative ones, people generally flourish. Psychologists involved in this research propose that people work towards 'positivity' ratios.

There is some variation in the ratios of positive to negative elements suggested if relationships are to be more PEA than NEA. Gottman3 has suggested 5:1, while Fredrickson and Losada[4] proposed 3:1. 5 The exact number is not as significant as realizing that significantly more time is needed in PEA if the benefits of that state are to be appreciated. In contrast, it takes extraordinarily little time for the deleterious costs of NEA to be observed. To understand why a detour into the brain's anatomy and how parts of it work is necessary.

The almond-shaped cluster of interconnected structures at the centre of all this is known as the amygdala. We have two amygdalae, one on each side of the brain, operating in all decision-making processes, especially when passion is part of the picture. It acts like a security guard sitting atop the tower through which the incoming signals from all our senses go. It is a sentinel scanning every experience for trouble—is this dangerous or something that could cause harm? If "yes," the amygdala reacts instantaneously, yelling crisis, putting all parts of the brain on alert. Doses of the hormone norepinephrine are released to heighten the reactivity of key brain areas, especially those that dial up the sensitivity of the senses. The fearful facial expression is also a result of the work of the amygdala in concert with parts of the brain stem. At the same time, the brain searches its memory banks for anything that might be useful to help deal with the matter at hand. As a matter of survival, this function takes precedence over everything else. When you are scared, you can't think of anything else.

Research has shown that the thalamus and its next-door neighbour, the amygdala, are the first places that sensory signals from the eyes and ears go.[6] From there, another call goes to the neocortex, the thinking part of the brain. It is a difference of milliseconds, but the amygdala has created an opinion about the signal in that short time. Essentially, you already feel something about what you've just heard or seen before you fully register and think about what your eyes or ears are telling you. A headstart like this is helpful if you run into a bear in the woods. You don't need to distinguish the type of claws or whether it is a brown or black bear before you get out of harm's way. That crunching sound with a bit of a grunt is enough for your amygdala to decide to give the source of that sound a wide berth. You can laugh about how much it was just a bird, so maybe you imagined the grunt afterwards you are far from danger. Your brain's design is to err on the side of caution. Better safe than sorry.

All of it builds up to this; whether the people mean it or not, we are prone to attaching some sinister motive to the look on their faces, tones, and words. It's better to get on the defensive quickly and protect yourself than get hurt. Abraham rebuked Abimelech. To rebuke is not just to feel you disapprove of someone's behaviour, but to express your displeasure, often in a critical way. Abimelech, however, was innocent. Where the patriarch assumed intent, Abimelech said it was the first he was hearing of it. How often has someone responded to something you didn't mean at all. How often have you been the one who misunderstood? Your amygdala puts you in NEA (fight or flight) mode, whether you misunderstood or someone else misunderstood you. You do what you can to feel safe again, and the lengths you go to reflect the level of threat you perceive at the time.

In his extensive study of the behaviour and language of couples (and other relationships), Gottman identified four patterns whose presence almost guarantees that a relationship is heading for ruin. They are so injurious to the future of any bond he has styled them the four horsemen like those in the book of Revelation. Criticism, contempt, stonewalling, and defensiveness interfere with effective communication, whether directly or indirectly expressed. Incredibly, in his practice of over two decades, having observed and studied over two hundred couples, Gottman predicted which couples seen in his lab would divorce within three years with 94 percent accuracy.[11] Over time, Gottman and his colleagues have found is that these horsemen are similarly devastating effects in all relationships, not just among the married.[8]

Practising

In times of anger and hurt, the horsemen may come in quick succession, one after the other. The negative emotional attractor state is full of fear and stimulates self-preservation, even if it comes through attacking someone else, which accomplishes the exact opposite of God's perfect love. In this state, complaints and hurts in this state come through without emotional intelligence but in a destructive fashion.

Typical indicators that someone is in NEA include lashing out with sarcasm and comments that include, "You're so..." It might be thoughtless, self-centred, worthless, lazy or whatever they see when they are feeling angry and hurt. It is destructive because it has gone beyond a complaint about the matter in question. Those words are tools of character assassination, critiquing the person, not the deed.

A complaint is a statement about a specific action and the feelings that it produces. It expresses foundational emotional intelligence: assertive, focused on the issue, not belligerent, passive or aimed at the other. Abraham may have said, "When your men seized my well and did not do anything about it, I felt like you no longer valued our friendship." It is formulaic and usable in any situation: *When you (whatever the action), it makes me feel like (emotion)."*

In contrast, personal criticism is what you hear when negative emotions are rampant and escalating toward a blind rage. "How can I trust you? You're so uncaring and always only think about yourself. It just proves what I've been saying- How can I expect you to do anything right?" Exercising some emotional intelligence now, how would the person on the other side of an attack like this feel? Ashamed, misunderstood, disliked, incapable, belittled- all the things that put them on the defensive. When it is one NEA against another, contempt builds.

From there, it goes beyond the words used. Raised voices to mock and insult; the rolling of the eyes; arms crossed, and finger-pointing are universal signs like curled or pursed lips. Contempt, criticism and defensiveness are also detectable in a tone of voice and an angry expression.

Of course, the occasional interaction with these elements will not break a marriage. However, if they are regular, the four horsemen bring destruction to the relationships. Gottman found that a wife with a habitually contemptuous and critical husband will be more prone to various health problems, including gastrointestinal symptoms (constipation, acid reflux), bladder and yeast infections, and frequent colds and flu. If a wife's face shows disgust (contempt's emotional cousin) four or more times in a fifteen-minute conversation, Gottman's work in over two decades shows the couple is likely to separate within four years. Over ninety percent of the time, these predictions prove accurate. Habitual criticism and contempt or disgust are dangerous because they reflect a state of mind, if not the heart. The husband or wife has forgotten that their spouse is only human, that things that hurt are mistakes, not items of deliberate design. They are no longer practising catching people doing right (Chapter 16). In their thoughts, their spouse is the subject of condemnation from which there is no redemption. A silent, continual judgment that sees only the worst in their partner is the default. Such negative and hostile thinking naturally leads to attacks, forcing their partner to be on the defensive constantly. The result is a cycle of exhausting shouting matches or pushing someone into stonewalling behaviours.

Stonewalling is the ultimate defensive posture, like a pangolin rolling into a tight, impenetrable ball. The stonewaller disengages and, in stony silence, offers nothing to the conversation. It is a powerful signal of distaste, a cold superiority that claims unmovable power. It says bend to my way, my will, or nothing. In Gottman's studies, stonewalling showed up mainly in marriages heading for trouble with the husband stonewalling in response to a wife who attacked with criticism and contempt in eighty-five percent of the cases. [14] Stonewalling may be the most devastating of the four as it cuts off all possibility of reconciliation.

Any time one of those four destructive behaviours occurs-contempt, criticism, defensiveness and stonewalling- the positivity ratios research suggests there have to be three to five positive interactions to cancel them out. Offer encouragement, genuine praise and authentic affirmation. Be generous with your resources, lavish with your compliments and say out loud those tiny things you notice but usually keep to yourself. Find ways to be useful and go out of your way to be helpful. Remember that Abraham brought animals as a peace offering, a sacrifice on his part so that it was clear that the well was his in the presence of witnesses.

Because these skills are difficult to call upon *during* confrontation when emotional arousal is sure to be high, you must overlearn them. Nothing else will make them accessible when they are needed most. In times of crisis, the emotional brain engages those responses we learned earliest in life. The amygdala has a unique ability to preserve emotionally rich memories so that what happens during repeated moments of anger and hurt become the dominant responses, even in adulthood. If a more effective emotional response is unfamiliar, it is tough to try it while upset.

Practice more emotionally intelligent responses. Practice giving people the benefit of the doubt. Approach misunderstandings with curiosity when the price for that miscommunication is low. Learn to bolster the abilities of others and promote cooperation through quality feedback and guidance. Practice them; try them out and rehearse them during encounters that are low stakes in nature and the heat of battle if they are to have a chance to become automatic.

Far more positive moments than negative ones says that an association has a good emotional bank account. It means you have to develop the ability to read and understand your emotions and recognize their impact on other people. A realistic evaluation of your strengths and limitations is also foundational to good relationships. Without these, you cannot come into relationships with curiosity or find the humility to admit it when you don't know something or when you are wrong. On the other hand, when you are open about what you are working on and invite your peers to help you develop, they are more likely to empathize with you. This is, in short, self-management.

Self-management is a characteristic skill of the most influential people regardless of their calling. Disruptive emotions are inevitable as long as you interact with others. It makes the ability to control your spirit, adjust to changing situations, and overcome obstacles necessary.

Abraham showed a propensity to de-escalate disagreements and orchestrate resolutions when dealing with Lot as their herdsmen fought over resources. Part of that was skill at sensing other people's emotions, understanding their perspectives, and taking an active interest in their concerns. Indeed, some of that ability came into play when he confronted Abimelech over his well. You will need to develop the same skills. You cannot fulfil your God-given purpose if you act on every impulse.

20

HIS CHILDREN AND
HIS HOUSEHOLD

Tradition teaches that the test God put Abraham through was about his "only son Isaac, whom you love." (Genesis 22:2) While it involved Isaac, it was not about him. A retrospective look at the story shows God was trying to tell Abraham (and us) how He would give His only begotten Son, whom He loves, for our salvation. This is true, but Abraham had no frame for reference. He didn't know God would stop Him at the last moment. Unfortunately, separating from or losing people he loved was a more common theme for Abraham than was comfortable:

1. He comes into the narrative at the end of Genesis Chapter 11, having lost his younger brother. He leaves Ur with his father and nephew. Soon after, Abraham loses his father.
2. Then God tells him to leave what's left of his family (which includes his brother Nahor).
3. By sheer force of their blessings, Lot, the one family member whom he arguably should not have even taken

along with in the first place, had to walk away because their herders were fighting.

4. Out of desperation for a son, his wife talked him into taking another woman so they could have a child. As soon as Hagar was pregnant, she picked up an attitude. Sarah responded with such harsh treatment that Hagar fled. Without the LORD's intervention in the wilderness, Abraham's hopes for a child would have gone with her.

5. Then, after Isaac was born, Sarah was at it again, telling Abraham to send his firstborn son, Ishmael, away. Now that Sarah had her son, Ishmael was no longer her son as her original plan was. It wasn't easy for him to do, even if God told Abraham to listen to Sarah's voice. In all of it, Abraham lost yet another person close to him.

Though not any less painful this time around, offering up Isaac would have been just another part of the story of Abraham losing people he loved. Save for Terah's death and the separation from Lot, God supported or started all the cases. This command to go and sacrifice Isaac was a test of love and priority. God tested Abraham:

➢ I promised you a son to be your heir, one who would be of your seed, through Sarah. I delivered on that promise. Now, I'm telling you to offer him up. Do you hold your promise closer to you and in higher esteem than you hold Me?

➢ Do you still trust Me to do what I said—set up my covenant through him—even if you don't see how?

➢ Will you walk with Me when the path I'm leading you on is a difficult one? Will you trust Me when you don't understand My commands?

➢ Will you fully surrender to Me, and obey, even if you would rather not do what I said?

We will all have to answer these questions in one form or another. It probably won't be the dramatic circumstances Abraham had to go through, but it will come. God is a jealous God, and He will not tolerate any other gods in your life. (Exodus 34:14) Abraham had to leave his ancestry behind because they were worshippers of idols carved out of wood, stone and metals. Idols take many forms these days, but they are still the same as in Genesis. Defined, a god is anything or anyone that causes you to doubt God, to take His commands lightly, anything you depend on more than Him. Your intellect, strengths, and abilities are included in that list when you rely on them rather than wield them in His service.

The Isaac test is about recognizing God's sovereignty over all things and giving Him the preeminent position in your life. It is having no attachment to anything more robust than your attachment to Him. It is loving nothing so dearly that you wouldn't give it up for Him. That includes your spouse and children. When God tested Abraham, part of the promise He had made when He called Abraham was still to come. He was in the land that God had shown him, but very much a stranger in it. Isaac was born, but the covenant had not been set up through him yet. If Abraham had not fully obeyed, he would have shortchanged himself in the fulfilment of God's promise. Likewise, the gifts you have- your job, spouse and children- are not everything God has for you.

God is your shield and covering. If you live fearfully, afraid your world will fall apart without your husband, you have made a god out of the gift and discarded the Giver. If your children or husband ultimately see you as their nurturer, their comforter, you have denied the El Shaddai (the Many-breasted One) His rightful place. He is jealous, a consuming fire (Deuteronomy 4:24) who insists, for your good, you fear the LORD your God, walk in all His ways, love Him, serve the LORD your God with all your heart and with all your soul. (Deuteronomy 10:12)

The test also speaks to giving attention and focus to the right things at the right time. To give your highest and best service to God and your family, you must first realize that this is a case of the compromise between the bread and baby. You cannot serve two masters is a theme repeated in this book. Loving and serving the Lord with half of yourself is to give no service at all. Marriage and parenting are also intolerant of partial dedication. You either love them entirely, or you don't love them. You are present with your spouse, or you are not. When you try to multitask, you are giving nothing your full attention. You have chosen to cut the baby in two, accept less and give less. Good decisions begin with distinguishing between priorities and posteriorities. Effective decision-makers know that posteriorities ought not to take up priorities' time and energy. They must get their own time in your schedule, if at all.[1]

Isaac was not a passive player in this drama. He would have been a young man, in his twenties or maybe even early thirties at the time. (Abraham was 100 years old when Isaac was born, and Sarah was ninety. She lived another 37 years after that.) Isaac would have been old enough for his father to put the wood for the burnt offering on him and travel together up the mountain after leaving the donkey behind.

> ➤ Why didn't he run away or offer up some other form of resistance once he found out he was to be the burnt offering?
> ➤ Would he have told his mother of his ordeal once they returned home?
> ➤ What was Sarah's role in all this? Did Abraham tell her what God had commanded before leaving for Moriah? If he did, did she let Isaac go willingly? Since she was so jealous and zealous for Isaac alone to inherit Abraham's wealth that she had Hagar and Ishmael expelled a second time, do we assume that she would have resisted? Or do we believe that since she laughed when God said she would

give birth in her old age, perhaps she wasn't as strong in her faith? If so, did Abraham tell her what happened after they got back?

Teaching and Learning

Regardless of the answers to these questions, this test reached beyond Abraham. It was a test for Isaac just as much. He would have grown up hearing the stories of his father's journey and the promises God had made. He was the son of promise, living proof God was faithful, that Isaac could trust Him. People often ask couples how they met, but the story among Abraham's contemporaries would have been about how Isaac was born. They talked about ministering to angels and the Lord visiting Sarah in her old age. Isaac's name reflected the joy he brought to his parents, who were both nearly 100 years old when he was born.

Now, he was about to die (again, neither of them knew God would stop the whole thing at the last minute). The command to sacrifice was a test of how well Abraham had commanded "his children and his household after him, that they keep the way of the LORD to do righteousness and justice, that the LORD may bring to Abraham what He has spoken to him." (Genesis 18:19) It was also a test of how well Isaac had learned those things. At that point, he would have matured in his faith. The LORD would have already been the God of Abraham and the God of Isaac. It would be quite the ordeal for him to be upon the altar, tied up and his father wielding a knife above him. Would he do that for his father's God, someone he had no relationship with on his own?

Together, it was a test of their faith as individuals, their conviction in God as a family, and the strength of Abraham and Sarah's marriage.

The call to sacrifice Isaac highlights that decision-making isn't about one person making choices. Just as giving people information is not teaching, picking between opinions is not decision-making. Any decision you make must open the door to a series of questions: who else needs to know about this decision? What actions do they need to take? Who needs to take that action? Are they equipped to do it well?

Teaching your vision and faith and confirming it is shared takes time. It is a process of engaging others in conversation about the hopes and dreams, listening, taking advice, having arguments and losing them sometimes and following others as much as leading. When there is a shared sense of destiny, everyone recognizes where they fit in stands up when it's their turn. The Lord appeared to Abraham and said, "Take now your son, your only son Isaac, whom you love, and go to the land of Moriah, and offer him there as a burnt offering on one of the mountains of which I shall tell you." (Genesis 22:2) Abraham knew what he had to do. When Isaac understood how he fit into that, he did not hesitate to subject himself to that mission. He understood he had a part to play somewhere along the way if God's promise to Abraham was to happen. Your family will need to show their understanding of your part in your vision and purpose.

Me and My House

It does no good to declare, "As for me and my house, we will serve the Lord" (Joshua 24:15) when your house doesn't know what you have committed yourself and them to. What do they need to do as part of that service? Who needs to do what? What role does your spouse need to play? What about the children? What are the expectations for each person? Does everyone know that is the standard against which their service is to be measured?

The decision to serve the Lord is great, but it is only the beginning. What would have happened if Sarah had said she didn't want to move at the very start? Would he have followed his heart and his Lord and left her behind? If he had, the story would have ended very differently. This happened with Lot when he and his family. His wife turned back against the given commands and famously turned into a pillar of salt. (Genesis 19:26) In the mountains, grief-stricken and under the focusing illusion, the girls plied their father with wine and fell pregnant by him. (Genesis 19:34-36) Lot's faith had not grown to become his family's faith.

Everyone must work out his salvation with fear and trembling. (Philippians 2:12) All members of that family were ultimately accountable to God for the lives He had given them and what they had done with them. As shown through the story of Eli, the high priest, there is an expectation that parents are accountable for the groundwork that their children can spring from as they begin their walk with the Lord. (1 Samuel 3:11-14) This expectation goes beyond family. The positions of managers, CEOs and coaches are not just about making decisions but seeing them implemented as well. When results are below the expected standard, organizations often replace their leaders because they could not share the vision so that everyone else could carry it out. You have worked on your values and defined your hedgehog concept. Share it with your family. Make sure they can see it too.

21

---◆———○———➤---

NEGOTIATING WHILE GRIEVING

Then Abraham stood up from before his death and spoke to the sons of Heth, saying, "I am a foreigner and a visitor among you. Give me property for a burial place among you, that I may bury my dead out of my sight." And the sons of Heth answered Abraham, saying to him, "Hear us, my lord: You are a mighty prince among us; bury your dead in the choicest of our burial places. None of us will withhold from you his burial place that you may bury your dead." (Genesis 23:3-6)

Though he was mourning, having lost the love of his life, Abraham did not let his grief overwhelm him. He had the wherewithal to carry out a business deal—procure a place to bury Sarah. Can you imagine what it would be like to have to shelve what you are feeling, having lost your life partner so that you can come into a negotiation with a level head?

We all must go about our daily business, and though we would prefer the world to stop or slow down a little while we grieve, it simply doesn't work that way. Nor is grief the only emotion we need to be able to suspend to go on living. The truth is it's not about stopping what we feel. It is about being able to do what we need to do *while* we grieve, feel hurt, angry, disappointed, disillusioned, shocked, weak, abandoned, helpless, defeated. God has not promised us a life without these.

Abraham was able to negotiate as adroitly as he did because of all the work he had unconsciously done ahead of time. He was living in a foreign land, yet, his interactions with them had been positive, cordial and collaborative. The Bible says the sons of Heth talked with him. He had friends people around him who respected and honoured him. (They say to Abraham, "You are a mighty prince among us," and refer to him as "my lord." Genesis 23:3-6) They saw his grief and understood it. They felt for him so much that Ephron tried to give him the land for free. Despite being in anguish, Abraham insisted on paying for the cave he wanted and not at a discounted price.

Two or more

If it is not good for man to be alone, the opposite is true. It is *terrific* for man to be connected to many others. Consider the many ways God has tried to get this point across. Jesus said, "where two or more are gathered in my name, there I am also. Whatever you ask Me for, if two or three agree together, it will be done unto you." (Matthew 18:19-20) The Lord inhabits the praise of His people. (Psalm 22:3) In each of these, the singular is also true. He will hear your prayer if you seek Him on your own. He is there if you praise Him alone. Connection with others, however, brings another level of experience. The issue is not the specific number stated; it is the concept of coming together with others.

Tuning into and growing your social network can pay you as great dividends as it did for Abraham. Again, the key is not just the number of people. The emphasis is on people with whom you can be vulnerable.[1] Researchers have made observations between relationships and the physical health of socially integrated people.

Being married, having close family and friends, belonging to social and religious groups, and participating in these networks were connected strongly with recovering more quickly from disease and living longer.[2]

Solid and diverse social connections also beget more trust as information flows more freely. Reciprocity increases, there is more collective action as people come together for common goals. In these groups, happiness ratings are higher, and there is more extraordinary wealth creation than in less diverse networks.[2] All of these are proven in Abraham's story, culminating in this negotiation for land. Abraham's ability in this area had these people stepping up when he needed them. "Hear us, my lord: You are a mighty prince among us. Bury your dead in the choicest of our burial places. None of us will withhold from you his burial place that you may bury your dead." They were not just offering him some piece of land somewhere. They surrendered their burial places, the best of them, just as Joseph of Arimathea would give up his tomb for Jesus. (John 19:38)

Private capital

How do you get people to want to give you the best of themselves and their stuff? By understanding that networks of personal contacts are a kind of private capital. Abraham's friendship was enough to get him the land. His friends loved and appreciated him that much. The money was to make the transaction formal, and by doing it with others watching, it became legally binding. With the Lord's favour over him, Abraham opened his tent to angels and the citizens around him, winning many friends along the way. Increasing his interconnectedness was part of God's plan to make Abraham a blessing and give him the land. Make building social connections a primary goal of yours.

Jesus relied on the generosity of the people he connected

with as He carried out His mission. There was "Joanna the wife of Chuza, Herod's steward, and Susanna, and many others who provided for Him from their substance." (Luke 8:3) Given that Zaccheus was willing to climb up a tree to get a glimpse, Jesus was confident He could invite Himself to his house. There he found good hospitality and possibly a place to sleep. (Luke 19:9) After ridding her of a fever, Peter's mother-in-law ministered to their needs. (Luke 4:38-39) The invitation, "Come see a man who told me everything I have ever done," resulted in a few days in Samaria. (John 4:29) People who had previously wanted nothing to do with Jews were happy to supply meals and shelter for Jesus and His disciples because they found having Him around was immensely beneficial. It meant salvation for the Samaritans because they believed He was the Messiah. "Foxes have holes, and the birds of the air have nests, but the Son of Man has nowhere to lay His head." (Matthew 8:20) Yet, He never went hungry or cold. People came to *Him* to have their needs met. That is the power of social connection, of having that ability to craft a question, empathize with others and turn strangers into friends.

Reaching your potential and completing your God-given mission is not just about the vastness of your network. Recall that Abraham refused to associate with the king of Sodom. Though he made friends with and lived among the Canaanites, he would not allow Eliezer to pick Isaac's wife from among them. It's not cosying up to everyone that is beneficial. The networks of top performers in any domain include people carefully chosen for a particular set of skills for excellence in some area. [3] These people trade and share their expertise and information in highly reciprocal, mutually beneficial relationships. Each person is an extension of knowledge and access to immediately available resources. People with these networks have a measurable, significant time advantage over those who have to use broader, more general sources of information to find answers. One estimate showed that for every hour spent seeking solutions through a network, an average person without an established network spends three to five hours gathering the same information.[4] Notably, these connections are built as a way of life. Like Abraham, the web will step up to help you need them, but if you wait until you need it before you build it, your experience will be much different from Abraham's.

Focus then on increasing the number of people in your life. Make new acquaintances while deepening your existing ones. Devote some time each day to expanding and building your connections into full-fledged friendships. They may not use the exact words, but if your friends think of you in the same terms that the sons of Heth thought of Abraham, you'll know you are doing well.

22

LEGACY

Abraham died at a good old age. His legacy is one for the ages. Muslims, Jews and Christians all trace their lineage back to him. Though he probably would not be pleased with the sibling rivalry between them, he would be overjoyed to see how much his seed has multiplied. He would be humbled and fall on his face before God, seeing how He had fulfilled His word. Abraham would be pleased with his decision when the Lord called him.

Living with your decisions is a crucial part of the decision-making process. Most advice on making better decisions stops when you have picked between your options. After that, you wait and see how things turn out. A better approach is to harness one of the keys to learning: feedback. If you want to learn anything quickly, optimize for feedback. Set things up to see how situations turn out each time you try. From each trial, have a process for figuring out the lessons. To apply this to decision-making, think about how you can get feedback on a decision *before* you implement it. It is a three-step process, beginning with understanding your influences, writing what you expect to happen and feedback analysis.

Understanding Your Influences

Only buy something you'd be pleased to hold if the market shut down for ten years. Warren Buffet's admonition considers the decision and what is influencing it. Expounding, he said, "For some reason, people take their cues from price action rather than from values. What doesn't work is when you start doing things that you don't understand or because they worked last week for somebody else. The dumbest reason in the world to buy a stock is because it's going up." 1 Because of the price, many move their money in and out of various stocks in the investing world.

Others do so based on the news headlines. Nassim Taleb demonstrated the folly of this approach in his book, the Black Swan.²

"On the day Saddam Hussein was captured (December 2003), Bloomberg News flashed the following headline at 13:01: *U.S. Treasuries Rise, Hussein Capture May Not Curb Terrorism.*

Whenever there is a market move, the news media feel obligated to give the "reason." Half an hour later, they had to issue a new headline. As these U.S. Treasury bonds fell in price (they fluctuate all day long, so there was nothing special about that), Bloomberg News had a new reason for the fall: Saddam's capture (the same Saddam). At 13:31, they issued the following bulletin: *U.S. Treasuries Fall; Hussein Capture Boosts Allure of Risky Assets.*

The headlines offered two opposing facts: the rise of treasuries and their fall thirty minutes later but used the exact cause to explain them. Saddam Hussein's arrest could cause them to go up or down, not both."

We can't help but prefer stories over raw truths, even if the narratives are illogical, like the headlines above. When looking at facts, our brains will have conjured some interpretation to explain what we are seeing before we know it. This tendency is known as the narrative fallacy. God's pronouncement, "It is not good for man to be alone" (Genesis 2:18), might be said for pieces of information too. The stories we form are relationships between facts, figures, or ideas, which makes them easy to recall when we need them. It helps them make more sense and makes them more easily accessible.

Accessibility means essential information can be retrieved and applied to various circumstances. Things go awry because all of this gives us the impression that we understand things better than we actually do. We think we know what's going on, and we think we know why, but this is often the work of unconscious processes. What is needed is a slowing down of the daily to bring some of the unconscious reasoning processes to consciousness.

Many of your decisions have that 'automatic' feeling to them. But having learned about substitution, perspective, and other influences, it is to your benefit to figure out what you *think* are the reasons for your decisions. A little like reverse-engineering, asking yourself, *Why do I believe that,* will yield some very instructive results.

God will test your faith as He did Abraham's. How will you respond? and he received a just reward for it. Though he grieved a tremendous loss, Job staunchly refused to attribute evil to God. He endured ridicule from his friends and had to reject terrible advice from his wife. All this happened because of what he understood to be the reason for his loss, "Lord gives, and the Lord takes." (Job 1:21) It kept him from overwhelm. It sustained as his grief, loneliness, confusion and hurt threatened to drown him.

Apply the effort to understand the beliefs that support your position. Write them down.

To get to those beliefs, you may have to take a hard look in the mirror and ask the relentless why question. Stringing 3 to 5 whys will help you find answers you might skim over if you choose not to record them. Here's an example.

Why am I thinking of starting my own company?
Answer: I would be happier doing my own thing than working for someone else.

Why would you be happier then?
Answer: I can have more control over all aspects of the business.

Why do you want more control?
Answer: I'm not happy with the lack of integrity where I work now.

There would be more questions to ask before starting your own business. Business owners must deal with responsibilities, dues, and sacrifices that are not plain to employees. However, this line of questioning would be something of a start to try and understand some of the motivations behind going out on your own.

Expectation Setting

When you have your reasons named and written down, write down, in an adjacent column, what you expect to happen and why. Abraham could say he believed God would set up His covenant through Isaac, so though the path past the burnt sacrifice was not clear, he still obeyed. He believed God could raise Isaac from the dead if necessary, so he bound him on the altar and was prepared to go through with the sacrifice. (Hebrews 11:19)

David believed Israel was the Lord's possession, the apple of His eye. Philistine taunting, threatening and attack was sure to provoke the anger of the Lord who would give Israel the victory. He felt there was transference both in the presence of the Lord and his skilful exploits as a shepherd. Because of that, he was willing to take on the Goliath without thinking he might fail. In the face of sword and spear, the name of the Lord of Hosts was armour enough. With five stones, David fully expected to win and collect the prize the king had promised. Events unfolded as he expected, and he was allowed to marry Michal. (1 Samuel 18:27)

Things won't always turn out the way you planned them. The narrative fallacy is a warning about how easy it is to create relationships where there are none or very slim correlations. It means things will work out sometimes, and it won't be for the reasons you think. Your approach may have contributed marginally or not at all. You may have been entirely wrong, but the outcome was still favourable. At other times, you will do everything you can and do it right, and things still won't turn out as you hoped. Writing down your motivations and expectations sets up the final stage of an approach called feedback analysis.

Feedback Analysis

Understanding your motivations helps you find clarity as to the why of your decision while the expectation setting is an attempt to say why you think te decision will will bring about the result you expect. Feedback analysis is a practice several months after you implement the decision.

Did things turn out the way you expected? Good decision makers know that outcomes and decisions are different things so they focus on the process that led to the decisions. There are significant event outside of your control that will impact the outcomes of any endevour. Luck and timing also play a big role.

Decision process + Luck and timing + outside events = outcome

Of the three, the decision process is the only one that is in your control. Feedback analysis is about learning what you can from a systematic study of how you make decisions. You can garner from that study what you are good at, where you show consistency, any weaknesses you might not otherwise be aware of and so on.

I have repeatedly referenced God's edict that it is not good for man to be alone. Feedback analysis can show you areas where you have weaknesses and for greater productivity, you may want to delegate work in those areas to someone else. Their efficiency will bring you results faster, and you will be able to work in an environment of less stress as everyone involved gets to work in and on those areas of their strengths.

Think about the energy, time and resources it would take for a student who is barely making a D grade to be able to achieve a C+. It will requires hours, tutoring, supplementary material and of course extra attention to get them to an acceptable pass grade, but nothing that will endear them to careers that require greater proficiency. A significant amount is poured in for a small return. What if that same student cut their losses, took all of those resources and applied them to getting even better at what they are already good at? Investment in this case leads to a much greater yield.

The world rewards specialization. That is how God designed it. He commissioned gifted artisans, filled with the spirit of wisdom and who could weave skillfully to make Aaron's garments for glory and for beauty. (Exodus 28:2-4). Anyone could have sown them, but God wanted specialists. He wanted similarly able men to work on the Tabernacle and everything that was to go into it. (Exodus 31:6-11) To figure out where you can and should specialize is why we discussed the three circles. It is why God calls you into the straight and narrow path. Feedback analysis is another tool you can use as you review your decisions. It is yours for creating a learning environment that brings more under your control giving you a better chance of getting the outcomes you want.

Your life is the product of your decisions (admittedly, others decided some things for you at various points). Your eternal destiny is undoubtedly going to be determined by your decision too. It makes it that much more vital that you are involved, not just in making the decisions that affect your life but in designing them too. When someone puts choices A, B and C in front of you, it is tempting to believe you have a choice. If you haven't had any part to play in deciding what A, B and C are, you are picking between someone else's options. Much of life will probably fall into this category. The suggestions throughout this book will help you make the best of a situation rigged to favour whoever decides what those choices would be.

However, when you can influence what is behind each door, you tip the scales in your favour. You give yourself the chance to be more productive, happier, and more fulfilled beyond the average. By taking the time to design your decisions, you can make more decisions you can live with and create a legacy worthy of your calling.

APPENDIX A

BROADEN YOUR EMOTIONAL VOCABULARY

Here, we'll look at nuance in questions that can aid you in your decision design if you are aware of it. Broadly, we define emotional intelligence (EI) as the ability to perceive your emotions and those of others and, through reflection, regulate those emotions. It also involves using those emotional experiences to inform positive adaptation[1,2]. The Lord's questions to Cain were essentially a test of his emotional intelligence. Because there is more of a conversation, and we can trace the link between emotion and behaviour, we will use Jonah's back-and-forth with God to discuss emotional differentiation.

The next time you are experiencing a strong emotion, take a moment to consider what to call it. For example, you might be happy. Don't stop there. Try to come up with two or three more words that describe your feelings. Are you the type of happy that you might dance in the street, regardless of what people might think, that you might hug a stranger? Or is it slightly more sedate but perhaps worth a whoop and punching the air? Or is it the silent kind of happiness of holding a newborn? There is also the tear-filled kind as you watch your child get baptized. You might say you are jubilant, joyful, beside yourself, excited, beaming, euphoric or delighted. There is so much to the depth of your experiences when you can describe them better, and possibly with that, deeper, more meaningful relationships.

Let's consider negative emotions to understand better how powerful it can be to broaden your emotional vocabulary. Ubiquitous though it may be in contemporary speech, 'stressed out' is not an emotion. When people use this term, they are using the most accessible descriptor to try and capture the general signs of the physiological stress response- increased tension everywhere and the awareness that your heart is beating faster thanks to an influx in adrenalin; heightened levels of alertness which mean you can pick up on every sound and movement. Your stomach might feel 'off', or you may be having those butterflies. These are appropriate changes to prepare the body to take on any perceived threats or get away from them. That may be at work as you interact with supervisors and bosses or work as you interact with your spouse or your children. It may be in response to the news or anticipation of driving into rush hour traffic. Because this is part of the *general* response to anything that may be a source of danger, feeling 'stressed out' reflects alexithymia—a difficulty that people have in accurately labelling their feelings so that they are constantly vague in expressing them.

Jonah

Having a more elaborate and precise lexicon is necessary because poorly diagnosing your feelings leaves you ill-prepared to respond to whatever might be going on. Using emotion-word labels to differentiate what you feel in a given moment conveys information about the situation and the various courses of action available[3]. Consider how difficult it must have been for Jonah. God had an assignment for him. "Arise, go to Nineveh, that great city, and cry out against it; for their wickedness has come up before Me"

(Jonah 1:2). Jonah knew that the Lord doesn't need permission to act, nor does He need to announce His intentions. If He wanted to destroy Nineveh, He would have done so. In Jonah's book, they deserved judgment and punishment. But if the Lord was sending *him* to deliver the message, this was not about a city getting its comeuppance. God's warning was, in effect, a show of mercy, a plea, and a directive for them to turn from their wicked ways. He intended to forgive them, not wipe them out. And Jonah, whose fellow Israelites had suffered historically at the hands of the Assyrians, was to go and extend the olive branch to his people's enemy right in their capital city. He wanted no part in it.

Jonah was deliberate in his direction and purpose. Tarshish was as far away from Nineveh as he could get. But we know Jonah doesn't make it there. A storm brews upon the sea, so powerful that all Jonah's fellow sailors thought prayer was the only salvation. Jonah knew it was from God, and soon he was in the water, in the belly of a great fish.

Stressed out could apply to work-related incidents, checking-in troubles at the airport, traffic, and Jonah's story. These cases, however, are not identical, demonstrating the impotence of using stressed out to describe how one feels in each. Emotions have a function. Intense feelings are more motivationally relevant- they give you more push to engage in active coping strategies. Guilt may signal that you have not lived up to one of your values- perhaps misbehaving towards others, while anger may signal that others have violated your expectations. Fear stops us from being comfortable in a potentially dangerous situation. Because of it, we take steps to address the threat or get to safety. When you are angry, feeling under pressure, and anxious about making your flight; when you are scared that your fellow sailors might find out their lives and livelihood are in danger because of you; when you are incredibly uncomfortable in the belly of a fish, embarrassed, humbled and worrying about how you are going to get yourself out of the mess you created, you will feel stressed. These other descriptors, however, are more pointed. Attached to the situation causing them, they are immediately more actionable. It is easier to know what to do next when you see what defines the problem well.

Remember the idea of defining the issue at its highest conceptual level. Because there is nothing new under the sun, every problem you face is another version of something already happened. It may even be something that you have encountered before. These examples show it is essential to be more granular about how you feel, and knowing why is useful too, especially if they are negative emotions. "Why are you cast down, O my soul? And why are you disquieted within me?" (Psalms 42:5) You will still have to have the self-awareness to answer the questions of your specific situations, but research has revealed an immensely beneficial aspect of emotions.

Emotions and core values

Our emotions, it seems, can also help us understand some of our core values.[3] This book is about your calling and how you can make more effective decisions that line up with that vocation. Research suggests that looking at your emotions through the lens of your values is a superior approach to focusing on your immediate feelings. Acting out of the latter often spurs poor decisions.

Let's look at Jonah and his mission to Nineveh once again.

Nineveh was the capital of Assyria, historically the enemy of God's people.

"Now the king of Assyria went throughout all the land, and went up to Samaria and besieged it for three years. In the ninth year of Hoshea, the king of Assyria took Samaria and carried Israel away to Assyria, and placed them in Halah and by the Habor, the River of Gozan, and in the cities of the Medes.

Then the king of Assyria brought people from Babylon, Cuthah, Ava, Hamath, and from Sepharvaim, and placed them in the cities of Samaria instead of the children of Israel, and they took possession of Samaria and dwelt in its cities. "(2 Kings 17:5-6, 24)

Some of this history was very recent, and its impact was still palpable when Jonah was an active prophet. You can understand his anger and resentment towards the Ninevites. Human nature demands some reparations before we are willing to forgive and forget. The prospect of being the one to deliver God's mercy wrapped up in the warning came from a feeling of injustice. Jonah felt that doing the impossible- running away from God- was better than giving a pass to his enemies for years of oppression.

The prayer Jonah offered from the belly of the fish seemed heartfelt and humble. He confessed his wrongdoing, and though he pleaded for God's mercy, he was not ready to forgive the Assyrians. When "God saw their works, that they turned from their evil way; and God relented from the disaster that He had said He would bring upon them, and He did not do it."

But it displeased Jonah exceedingly, and he became angry. So he prayed to the LORD and said, "Ah, LORD, was not this what I said when I was still in my country? Therefore I fled previously to Tarshish; for I know that You are a gracious and merciful God, slow to anger and abundant in lovingkindness, One who relents from doing harm. Therefore now, O LORD, please take my life from me, for it is better for me to die than to live!" Jonah 3:10-4:3

Jonah said he would rather die than live in a world where God forgave his enemies. Those things that Jonah knew about, loved and depended on God for were the same ones that sent him into a fit of anger so strong that he asked to die. The only difference was that God chose to extend those same qualities- to people who needed justice and vengeance, as Jonah saw it. Would Jonah have acted this way if he had been aware that his bias was the problem? Would he have been so angry if he knew it was his refusal to forgive that God's assignment was designed to expose? The record doesn't tell us how Jonah responded to God's final question. Hopefully, what the Lord demonstrated using that plant helped Jonah repent and take a more compassionate stance towards the Ninevites.

Your values need always to be in the foreground. Like a compass that guides you on your journey, you need to check with them often if you are going to stay on the right path. Your emotions can help with that. Just as anger was, in Jonah's case, was an indicator that the Ninevite assignment threatened his sense of justice, what you feel is an indicator of something important to you. When you look at it this way, you realize that managing your emotions is not pretending you don't feel or stuffing them away. Instead, it is asking yourself, how well does this action line up with your value? Does not having that difficult conversation bring you closer or further away from creating a close, supportive family? Does caving in to your anxieties and insisting on controlling everything demonstrate your faith in God's provision? Asking how the action you are contemplating reflects your values free you from the thrall of your feelings at the moment and steers you towards more value-consistent choices.

Because there is nothing new under the sun, you will have to deal with things repeatedly. Asking questions that seek to develop better congruency between what you do and what you value can be helpful. To make better decisions, you'll want to set up strategies that let you use your emotions constructively rather than letting them be the arbiter of your actions and behaviours. Over time, you will be able to uncouple your feelings from destructive outbursts, tantrums, sulking and possibly more sinister activities. Until then, you have to develop a habit of reflecting on moments of intense emotion.

If you look at what happened and why you acted as you did, you can learn much. Returning briefly to the 80/20 idea, what were the conditions when you felt a powerful positive emotion? What were you doing? Who was there, and what did they contribute?

See if you can create an environment (schedule, work or home cadence and tone) that allows for more.

If it was a negative emotion, what happened? Why did you act the way you did? Do you need to talk to someone and repair a relationship? These questions can help turn regrettable situations into opportunities for better, stronger relationships and act more like you'd like when a similar issue comes back. Returning then to labelling your emotions well- what would you do if you shifted from stressed out to angry? Hopefully, your first step is to pinpoint what you are mad about. Sometimes we get mad because of how someone said something even though the content of their words was sound. The value of this type of discrimination is obvious- you can absorb the criticism or correction and address its delivery.

Note that these are reflective questions. Resist the urge to be overly analytical. If you try to break down every detail, you will only flame the sense of injustice, unfairness, anger, and desire to get even. You will, in effect, be taking counterproductive steps.[4] Focus is a stimulus for growth. So approach your reflections with a more solution-oriented lens than a diagnostic who-is-to-blame one. As we've seen with Abraham, it's the relationship that's most important. What do you like about the person involved? What do you want for your relationship? Focus on that, and the course you'll take to resolve the anger will be more like my to achieve just that.

▌ Emotional Differentiation in Practice

Training on emotion differentiation has excellent benefits for anyone in a position of influence. Parents, coaches on sports teams or even leaders at work will appreciate the outcomes of several vital experiments.

Research shows that on questions of morality, incidental emotions have much less influence on the judgements of people skilled at making fine distinctions between emotions than those less skilled[5]. For example, when people were exposed to noxious smells and then asked to make judgments on various scenarios, they were more severe in their condemnation of things they thought were immoral[6]. Drinking something disgusting had a similar effect- it made people harsher in moral judgments6.

These effects are minimal in people who have some training in distinguishing between emotional experiences. Researchers think this is because they have a better awareness of the sources of their emotional experiences[7]. In other words, they can tell when what they are feeling is relevant to their task, and when they are not, they can resist the biasing impact emotions can have. These findings translate into everyday situations.

Many of the things that contribute to a problematic or toxic work culture are because we are likely to mislabel someone else's emotions as our own. When we bring negative outlooks into the office, it is easy to take innocent, off-the-cuff comments to heart. We may give unnecessarily harsh feedback. Or, when receiving feedback, focus only on the things that we hear are going wrong. Both have similarly complicated consequences. Imagine being able to concentrate and perform your tasks rather than produce sub-standard work as you ruminate over an incident that happened in traffic. Much of the striving from work makes its way home, making for unpleasant conversations with spouses. By understanding what they are feeling more precisely, you will be better able to respond constructively.

Parents often run into moments of impatience or yelling as their young children incessantly ask for things or perhaps have tantrums. Hunger stimulates the sympathetic nervous system, mobilizing the body for finding food. The hormones associated with that are the same, making us irritable and likely to have an outburst. Would it be helpful if they could tell that they are hungry (and perhaps their children as well?).

When a person struggles to manage intense distress, life aims such as having an enduring marriage, being a compassionate parent, and whatever else God has called you to become secondary to emotional-regulation efforts quickly. Once that happens, those who struggle with emotion differentiation and regulation spend more time chasing calm, quietness, control or blocking out overwhelming emotions. They are likely to engage in responses that (might) make them feel better but are ultimately poorly tailored to the situation and often unhealthy. Examples include binge drinking, so called-emotional eating, smoking and aggression in their speech and perhaps even physically.[8]

In contrast, people with the skill to verbally characterize their emotional experiences with granularity and detail find stressful situations[9] easier to manage. They can extract information about the case and the values under threat. The labelled emotions become easier to regulate and either become irrelevant or facilitate a person's finding appropriate and creative means to deal with whatever they are striving with[10]. With healthy management of emotions, a person can better pursue what's important to them.

This research suggests that precision and clarity in labelling your emotions is a worthy goal. Even if you cannot find the perfect word, the attempt alone motivates you to better regulate what you feel.

APPENDIX B

APPLYING THE DECISION DESIGN MODEL

I had the opportunity to put this model to the test, and I found the results surprising at the very least.

The Lord blessed me with a small but significant amount of money, and immediately, I thought about the parable of the talents. How could I multiply it? How could I be one of the good and faithful servants?

All sorts of reasons cause people to sell their businesses, and retirement was the impetus for the one that caught my eye. Two older women, each citing it was time to hang it up and spend more time with their grandchildren, had listed their life's work for sale. They were selling a profitable business serving people a sweet tooth for almost twenty years. Their asking price was within my price range, and it was in a town where I have some family. That appealed to me very much, and if I was to reveal all my reasons, the potential to write off holiday trips as business ones come tax time whetted my appetite even more. If I kept my job so that this purchase was an investment, I could influence but otherwise watch from a distance. I could reap its harvest, "topping up" my other salary to allow us a few more opportunities to live life to the fullest. Having grown up without my father, the topmost among those opportunities would be to be present for the important things in my children's lives. I relish not having to choose between being at work and being there to teach them to ride their bikes, throw a ball, and even play with some blocks. Owning the shop would get me started on my desire to own businesses that will be conduits to the other callings of my life. There was every reason to go for it.

But was it the *right* investment option? Or did it seem like the right one because it was the first one that had appealed to me when I had cast the net? The recency effect and the availability heuristic were on my mind. Their influence on decision-making and behaviour is strong, and I wanted to examine the situation with a broader lens.

I began with a simple question: is the chocolate shop the right investment?

Within moments of writing that down, a second question came to me that I hadn't even considered yet: what makes an investment choice right/good? A concise list appeared:

1. Low price, high value
2. Highest possible ROI (why shouldn't I expect my investment to be returned to me tenfold?)
3. Does it have a high probability of returning that investment 10X instead of simply having the possibility? After all, all things are possible.
4. Low-risk level

If I were to become objective, I would need to go beyond myself, lest this list is just the primary criteria I knew this shop already met. So I did some research and expanded my list a little.

1. The best investments are assets that increase in value over time.
2. Company values increase when they reinvest profits to increase ability.

3. Illiquid investments are less volatile.
4. The best long-term investments have a steady, continuous yield.
5. The power of an asset to generate sustainable cash proves it is profitable.

All this falls under Rule #1 in the decision matrix—what needs to LAST (be Looked At, Studied, Tested). With these criteria, I had something to put the chocolate shop against to open my eyes beyond the bias I already had because I was interested in buying it.

The last point, the idea of sustainable cash flow, stuck with me more than the others. These criteria helped me vet the financials a little more and ask more poignant questions of the sellers. What was surprising for me was the realisation at the same time that perhaps the reason I wanted to invest in the first place was feeling the need for more cash flow in my life. So I explored that more: Why do I want to invest first? And to boot, how are we defining "investment?"

The answers to these two questions were the deciding factors. First, I wanted to invest because I wanted to ensure I had enough money stowed away, working for me, to support my family. Beyond food and shelter, I also realised I wanted resources, opportunities, and time. To be there for my children is a question of time, not money. It can be burdensome to have a conversation for half an hour over how much getting new socks for the kids or colour pencils will derail the budget. What I wanted to get from my investments was the *ability to order my priorities as I saw fit to enhance my quality of life.* To have the financial side taken care of through those investments would take money off the top of the list. These are not new questions at all. There is nothing unique about them. As far as the class of my problem goes, it is pretty generic, and that means if the answer is not readily available, finding it would not be difficult.

An investment, it turned out, was whatever I was willing to do now to be able to order my priorities as I wanted. "Unless a grain of wheat falls into the ground and dies, it remains alone; but if it dies, it produces much grain" (John 12:24). In the season that grain is in the ground, it does not count among the ones available to eat. In other words, where was I willing to give up something now and suffer the discomfort of that temporary loss for something better in the future? The key ideas here were quick, pain, better and future. These also needed definition, and I weighed them on the scales of my values. As I did my due diligence, I found a few things that swayed my decision:

> The potential for a return several times my investment was still probable, but it was low.
> I would have to put much time into the business to realise that low return, learning its nuances. With a job that already consumes so much of my time to make me think I need to reorder my priorities, taking on another would give me even less time with my family.
> Less time with my family, perhaps for a decade or more, for a low return with which I would barely be able to make a dent into the other areas of my calling.

One of the key elements of decision-making is asking this question: can I live with this? At this point, the answer was no. These days, the formative years of my sons' lives are not ones I'd like for them to see so little of me that they might think or feel like I did when my father wasn't around. Trading my assignment to command my children and my household after me, that they keep the way of the LORD, to do righteousness and justice for a chance to make more money is not my definition of investment. Shall I work harder and longer now, never being there with and for them, to make money I may not get to spend with them because they have grown up without my example, instruction and guidance? No.

Rule number 2 is, "Always assume the other person is intelligent, reasonable and tenable." I was in the field of human kinetics when we met, studying the way the body moves, its anatomy, physiology and psychology. These added to my bachelor's degree for what would become a career in rehabilitation. It was while I was a rehabilitation specialist that I considered this investment. My wife felt that investing was the right idea, but this shop was not the right one. She had never known me in any other role and thought I'd be tethered to it if I bought a chocolate shop, and somehow it became my full-time work. I would have none of the excitement and sense that I excel at something.

My vision for the shop involved her and her talents in cooking and baking. We could make it work with a few employees and my leadership—the transferable skill I'd bring to all this. But after finding out that the current state of the shop was due to both owners working, sometimes 40+ hours a week, I was less enthusiastic. Coupling that with the time demands both on my children and my marriage, on top of my already full-time job managing a growing number of clinics in my role as president of clinical services, there was more to be invested here than just money. I found I was answering the original question: is this the right investment choice? "Yes, provided that…." Those caveats were the deciding factor. They took the enthusiasm from a yes with my whole heart, mind and soul to something less.

Having gone through building a business from scratch before, I know there is no investment without risk. There is no success in anything without having to struggle through some stuff. The stories of people who say they made it to the top by using the obstacles as steppingstones are aplenty. I said no to the chocolate shop opportunity, not because I was looking for a unicorn, a business that did not require sacrifice. I was looking, however, for something where the cost (financial and otherwise) was one I was happy to pay. My family is not an acceptable cost for a little more money, a bit more comfort and an extra holiday or two—neither now nor in the future. What shall it profit a man from gaining the whole world and losing his soul? (Mark 8:36)

However, the lessons from applying the model to a real-life decision were not whether the matrix is usable or not. They lay in what I saw in the process:

> The way you frame the question is crucial to the outcome of the process. Therefore, don't phrase your inquiry to have a binary yes or no solution. Instead, add some objectivity to your question by turning it into a "what" question. Is this a worthwhile investment opportunity changes to, What makes an investment opportunity "good?"

> What criteria must this decision meet to make it the right course of action?

> What needs to be accurate and a fact (not an opinion) for this to be the better possibility?

> Unfortunately, because so many factors affect the outcomes of any situation, we often "get away" with poor decisions. Any decision made without carefully considering and defining the problem and its network of influence will be a poor decision.

Most important on that list are the *people*. In Appreciative Inquiry, practitioners suggest not just telling people about decisions but also involving them in the process. People who participate in the discussions in arriving at decisions are far more likely to champion them, support them, and help their leaders see them through. In other words, there is less resistance to a decision. Including them gives them a sense of ownership, not just in the decision but also in the outcome. This may not be doable all the time, but having people presented and their opinions heard will always be of benefit.

The Bible doesn't give us much detail about how much Abraham included Sarah in what they were going to do. It took much faith for her to subordinate herself to his leadership and do as he asked (which in most cases was merely God's command),

and that is, in itself, a window into the nature of their relationship. There was trust between them. They shared the marriage bond, and they could say their heart's deepest desire was the same. In the absence of those things, the story of Abraham might read very differently, right from the move from Uz.

For this reason, though she would often bring up the opposite side of what I was seeing, my wife would always be a part of the decision-making process. My vision for the shop depended on her creativity and skill in the kitchen.

Essential questions to ask therefore include:

➢ Who else will be affected by this decision?
➢ What are the significant factors in their perspective that might make this a good decision? How will this affect them?

There are other factors to this concept. All of them add weight to the most powerful lesson: making good decisions is more about having high-quality questions that produce more clarity about the situation. Only then can you arrive at effective decisions.

END NOTES

Introduction

1   Lapin, Daniel E. *Thou shall prosper.* Hoboken, N.J.: John Wiley & Sons, 2010

Chapter 1: Calling and Purpose

1   Rabbi Daniel Lapin. (2014) Business Secrets from the Bible: Spiritual Success Strategies for Financial Abundance. Lapin, Daniel E. *Thou shall prosper.* Hoboken, N.J.: John Wiley & Sons, 2010

Chapter 2: Settings a Vision

1   Gilbert, D. T., and Wilson, T. D. (2007). Prospection: experiencing the future. *Science* 317, 1351–1354. DOI 10.1126/science.1144161
2   Hill, P. L., and Turiano, N. A. (2014). Purpose in life as a predictor of mortality across adulthood. Psychol. Sci. 25, 1482–1486. DOI 10.1177/09567976145 31799
3   Dobrow Riza, S., and Heller, D. (2015). Follow your heart or your head? A longitudinal study of the facilitating role of calling and ability in the pursuit of a challenging career. J. Appl. Psychol. 100, 695–712. DOI 10.1037/a0038011
4   Boyatzis, R. E., and Akrivou, K. (2006). The ideal self as the driver of intentional change. J. Manag. Dev. 25, 624–642. DOI 10.1108/02621710610678454
5   Ibid.

6   Boyatzis RE, Rochford K and Taylor SN (2015) The role of the positive emotional attractor in vision and shared vision: toward effective leadership, relationships, and engagement. Front. Psychol. 6:670. DOI 10.3389/fpsyg.2015.00670

7   Baumeister, R. F., Bratslavsky, E., Finkenauer, C., and Vohs, K. D. (2001). Bad is stronger than good. Rev. Gen. Psychol. 5, 323–370. DOI 10.1037/10892680.5.4.323

8   Chuang, S. C., and Lin, H. M. (2007). The effect of induced positive and negative emotion and openness-to-feeling in student's consumer decision making. J. Bus. Psychol. 22, 65–78. DOI 10.1007/s10869-007-9049-6

9   Heaphy, E. D., and Dutton, J. E. (2008). Positive social interactions and the human body at work: linking organizations and physiology. Acad. Manag. Rev. 33,137–162. DOI 10.5465/AMR.2008.27749365

10   Levenson, R. W. (1992). Autonomic nervous system differences among emotions. Psychol. Sci. 3, 23–27. DOI 10.1111/j.1467-9280.1992.tb00251.x

11   McEwen BS & Lasley EN 2002 The End of Stress As We Know It. Washington, DC, USA: Joseph Henry Press.

12   VandeWalle, D., Brown, S. P., Cron, W. L., and Slocum, J. W. Jr. (1999). The Influence of goal orientation and self-regulation tactics on sales performance: a longitudinal field test, J. Appl. Psychol. 84, 249–259. DOI 10.1037/00219010.84.2.249

Chapter 4: Is this what you promised me?

1   Drucker, P. F. (2006). The effective executive. HarperCollins.

2   Kahneman, D. (2011). Thinking, fast and slow. Farrar, Straus and Giroux.

3   Warren Buffett, Berkshire Hathaway, CEO

Chapter 5: That I may live because of you

1   Deborah J. Mitchell, J. Edward Russo, Nancy Pennington, Back to the Future: Temporal Perspective in the Explanation of Events, Journal of Behavioral Decision Making, 2, 25-38 (1989).

2   Gary Klein, Performing a Project Premortem, Harvard Business Review, 2007; available at <https://hbr.org/2007/09/performing-a-project-premortem&gt

3   David, S. (2016). *Emotional Agility: Get Unstuck, Embrace Change, and Thrive in Work and Life*. New York: Avery/Penguin Random House.
4   Barrett, L. F. (2017). *How emotions are made: The secret life of the brain*. Houghton Mifflin Harcourt.
5   Pinker, S. (2011). *The better angels of our nature: Why violence has declined*. New York: Viking.
6   Kahneman, D. (2011). *Thinking, fast and slow*. Farrar, Straus and Giroux.

Chapter 6: Conflict Resolution

1   Drucker, P. F. (2006). The effective executive. HarperCollins.

Chapter 7. Boundaries and costs

1   van Dijk, and Rik Pieters, "The Inaction Effect in the Psychology of Regret," Journal of Personality and Social Psychology 82 (2002): 314–27.
2   Berkshire Hathaway Annual Report, 1996.

Chapter 8: Right People, Right Seats

1   California Department of Mental Health, Friends Can Be Good Medicine (San Francisco: Pacificon Productions, 1981); and E. M. Hallowell, Connect: Twelve Vital Ties That Open Your Heart, Lengthen Your Life, and Deepen Your Soul (New York: Pocket Books, 2001).
2   A Ross, "Does Friendship Improve Job Performance? * Harvard Business Review March-April 1977), and K. A. Jehn and P. P. Shah, "Interpersonal Relationships and Task Performance: An Examination of Mediating Processes in Friendship and Acquaintance Groups," Journal of Personality and Social Psychology 72, no. 4 (1997): 775-790.
3   L. F. Berkman and S. L. Syme, "Social Networks, Host Resistance, and Mortality: A Nine-Year *
4   Follow-Up Study of Alameda County Residents," American Journal of Epidemiology 109, no. 2 (1979): 186-204; and S. Cohen, "Psychosocial Models of the Role of Social Support in the Etiology of Physical Disease, Health Psychology 7 (1988): 269-297.
5   Vu, R. 2016. Achieving Peak Performance: A Conversation with Anders Ericsson. Available at https://behavioralscientist.org/achieving-peak-performance-a-conversation-with-anders-ericsson/

6   Collins, J. (2001). Good to great. Random House Business Books.

7   Koch, R. (1998). 80/20 principle. New York: Currency

8   Buffet, W. CEO, Berkshire Hathaway.

9   Hoffman, BG. What is Red Teaming? https://www.redteamthinking. com/what-is-red-teaming

10 Schawbel D. (2017). How to make your organization flatter and more connected: An Interview with Chris Fussell. Available at https://www.forbes.com/sites/danschawbel/2017/06/13/chris-fussell-how-to-make-your-organization-flatter-and-more-interconnected/?sh=730bf336789e

11 McChrystal, S. (2015) I Don't Have a Secret Formula for Hiring, But I'll Ask This Question About Self-Awareness. Available at https:// www.linkedin.com/pulse/how-i-hire-dont-have-secret-formula-hiring-ill-ask-stan-mcchrystal

Chapter 9: The Discipline of No

1   Collins, J. (2001). Good to great. Random House Business Books.

2   Isaacson, W. (2015). Steve Jobs. Abacus.

3   Drucker, P. F. (2006). The effective executive. HarperCollins.

Chapter 10: Your Exceedingly Great Reward

1   Kahneman, D. (2011). *Thinking, fast and slow*. Farrar, Straus and Giroux.

Chapter 11: He Believed

1   Sinek, S. (2017). *Leaders eat last*. Portfolio Penguin.

2   Kouzes, J. M., & Posner, B. Z. (2012). The Leadership Challenge (5th ed.). Hoboken, NJ: John Wiley & Sons.

AChapter 12: Simplify

1   Slovic, P., & Corrigan, B. (1973). Behavioral problems of adhering to a decision policy. In Tsai, C. I. et al., Effects of amount of information on judgment accuracy and confidence, Organizational Behavior and Human Decision Processes (2008), DOI 10.1016/j.obhdp.2008.01.005

Chapter 13: When bad ideas seem good

Greimel at al. (2018) Arch Orthop Traum Surg 136:1639

Han, E. (2018). Doctors advised to stop performing arthroscopic surgery for osteoarthritis. https://www.smh.com.au/healthcare/doctors-advised-to-stop-performing-arthroscopic-knee-surgery-for-osteoarthritis-20180202-h0sna1.html

Chapter 16: Generosity is Godlikeness

1, 2 Lapin, Daniel E. (2010) Thou shall prosper. Hoboken, N.J.: John Wiley & Sons

Chapter 17: Looking for the right

1   Rath, T. (2015). Fully charging your life and work. In Lewis, S. (2016). Positive psychology and change: How leadership, collaboration, and appreciative inquiry create transformational results. Wiley-Blackwell. https://doi.org/10.1002/9781118818480

2   Achor, S. (2011). The happiness advantage: The seven principles of positive psychology that fuel success and performance at work. New York, NY: Random House.

Chapter 18: Assumptions and Emotions

1   Kahneman, D. (2011). *Thinking, fast and slow.* Farrar, Straus and Giroux.

2   Daniel Gilbert and Timothy D. Wilson, "Miswanting: Some Problems in Affective Forecasting," in Feeling and Thinking: The Role of Affect in Social Cognition, ed. Joseph P, Forgas (New York: Cambridge University Press, 2000), 178-97.

Chapter 19: Covenental Conversation

1   Gottman, J. M., Murray, J. D., Swanson, C. C., Tyson, R., and Swanson, K. R. (2002). The Mathematics of Marriage: Dynamic Non-Linear Models. Cambridge, MA: MIT Press.

2   Baumeister, R. F., Bratslavsky, E., Finkenauer, C., and Vohs, K. D. (2001). Bad is stronger than good. Rev. Gen. Psychol. 5, 323–370. DOI 10.1037/1089-2680.5.4.323

3   Gottman, J. M. (1994). What Predicts Divorce? The Relationship Between Marital Processes and Marital Outcomes. Hillsdale, NJ: Lawrence Erlbanm.

4   Fredrickson, B. L., and Losada, M. F. (2005). Positive affect and the complex dynamics of human flourishing. Am. Psychol. 60, 678–686. DOI 10.1037/0003066X.60.7.678

5   Cameron, K. S. (2008). Paradox in positive organizational change. J. Appl. Behav. Sci. 44, 7–24. DOI 10.1177/0021886308314703

6   John A. Bargh, "First Second: The Preconscious in Social Interactions. In Goleman, D. (1995). Emotional intelligence: Why it can matter more than IQ. New York: Bantam Books.

7   Joseph LeDoux, "Emotional Memory Systems in the Brain," Behavioural Brain Research, 58,1993; Joseph LeDoux, "Emotion, Memory and the Brain," Scientific American, June, 1994; Joseph LeDoux, "Emotion and the Limbic System Concept," Concepts in Neuroscience, 2, 1992.

8   Gottman, J. (1995). Why marriages succeed or fail: And how you can make yours last. New York: Simon and Schuster.

9   Gottman, J. (1999). The seven principles for making marriage work. New York: Three Rivers.

Chapter 20: His children and his household

1   Drucker, P. F. (2006). The effective executive. HarperCollins.

Chapter 21: Negotiating while grieving

1   Goleman, D. (2013). Focus: The hidden driver of excellence. Bloomsbury.

2   Gladwell, M. Tipping Point.

3   Baker, W. Achieving Success through social capital: Tapping the Hidden Resources in Your Personal and Business Networks. San Francisco: Jossey-Bass, 2000.

4   Kelley, RE. (1998) *How to Be a Star at Work*. New York: Times Books.

Chapter 22: Legacy

1   Taleb, N. N, (2007). The Black Swan: The impact of the highly improbable. New York: Random House.

Appendix A

1   Salovey, P., & Mayer, J. D. (1990). Emotional Intelligence. Imagination, Cognition and Personality, 9(3), 185–211. https://doi.org/10.2190/DUGG-P24E-52WK-6CDG
2   Salovey, P., & Sluyter, D. J. (Eds.). (1997). *Emotional development and emotional intelligence: Educational implications.* Basic Books.
3   Barrett, L. F. (2006b). Solving the emotion paradox: Categorization and the experience of emotion. Personality and Social Psychology Review, 10, 20–46.
4   **David, S. (2016). Emotional Agility: Get Unstuck, Embrace Change, and Thrive in Work and Life.**
5   Cameron, C. D., Payne, B. K., & Doris, J. M. (2013). Morality in high definition: Emotion differentiation calibrates the influence of incidental disgust on moral judgments. *Journal of Experimental Social Psychology, 49*(4), 719–725. https://doi.org/10.1016/j.jesp.2013.02.014
6   Schnall, S., Haidt, J., Clore, G. L., & Jordan, A. H. (2008). Disgust as Embodied Moral Judgment. Personality and Social Psychology Bulletin, 34(8), 1096–1109. https://doi.org/10.1177/0146167208317771
7   Eskine, K. J., Kacinik, N. A., & Prinz, J. J. (2011). A bad taste in the mouth: gustatory disgust influences moral judgment. *Psychological science, 22*(3), 295–299. https://doi.org/10.1177/0956797611398497
8   John, O. P., & Gross, J. J. (2004). Healthy and unhealthy emotion regulation: personality processes, individual differences, and life span development. *Journal of personality, 72*(6), 1301–1333. https://doi.org/10.1111/j.1467-6494.2004.00298.
9   Kashdan, T. B., Barrett, L. F., & McKnight, P. E. (2015). Unpacking Emotion Differentiation: Transforming Unpleasant Experience by Perceiving Distinctions in Negativity. Current Directions in Psychological Science, 24(1), 10–16. https://doi.org/10.1177/0963721414550708
10 Tamir, M. (2009). What do people want to feel and why? Pleasure and utility in emotion regulation. Current Directions in Psychological Science, 18, 101–105.

CPSIA information can be obtained
at www.ICGtesting.com
Printed in the USA
BVHW040051220522
637687BV00001B/7

9 781664 264830